GOD
HAS NOT FORGOTTEN
ABOUT YOU

Books by
Leslie Haskin
FROM BETHANY HOUSE PUBLISHERS

Between Heaven and Ground Zero
God Has Not Forgotten About You

GOD
HAS NOT
forgotten ABOUT
YOU

...AND HE CARES MORE THAN YOU CAN IMAGINE

LESLIE HASKIN

BETHANYHOUSE
MINNEAPOLIS, MINNESOTA

Published by Bethany House Publishers
11400 Hampshire Avenue South
Bloomington, Minnesota 55438

Bethany House Publishers is a division of
Baker Publishing Group, Grand Rapids, Michigan.

Printed in the United States of America

In keeping with biblical principles of creation stewardship, Baker Publishing Group advocates the responsible use of our natural resources. As a member of the Green Press Initiative, our company uses recycled paper when possible. The text paper of this book is comprised of 30% post-consumer waste.

Library of Congress Cataloging-in-Publication Data

Haskin, Leslie D.
    God has not forgotten about you : —and he cares more than you can imagine / Leslie Haskin.
        p.   cm.
    Summary: "Presents biblical insights and personal stories to consider when common challenges and unmet longings in life threaten to erode one's faith"—Provided by publisher.
    ISBN 978-0-7642-0604-7 (pbk. : alk. paper) 1. Consolation. 2. Christian life. I. Title.

BV4905.3.H383   2009
248.8'6—dc22

                                                                2008052075

DEDICATION

First, I thank God that He has allowed me once again to represent His kingdom.

This book is dedicated to the strong women in my life . . . those who endure: my aunt Leontyne and Mother Bolden. The sisters who my mother gave me: Lanita, Gal, Mabel, LaVerne, Lanette, and Lenore. The sisters my brothers brought into my life: Sylvia, Coletta, and Delia. Those I found on my own: Veva, my soul's twin; Adrienne, Melissa, and Shannon. And finally to my nieces: Lesa, Mickey, Shawn, Nina, Lauren, Shauntina, and Quiana.

I pray for all of you . . . that you would know that God's grace in your lives is evidence of His presence in your lives! Be encouraged in your everyday walk with our Father.

ABOUT THE AUTHOR

LESLIE HASKIN has become the voice of hope for many since her miraculous escape from the World Trade Center on September 11, 2001. She wrote about that experience in *Between Heaven and Ground Zero* (Bethany House, 2006). Today, Leslie is active in outreach ministry and is the founding director of Safe HUGS, an agency that helps victims of domestic abuse. She makes her home in upstate New York. To learn more about Leslie, or schedule her to speak at your next event, visit *www.lesliehaskin.net*.

A NOTE TO YOU, MY READER

The day begins in a sweet quietness. It's early, the birds are chirping outside, and my coffee is hot. I walk onto my deck, blow over the top of my cup, and watch my breath meet the open air. It's familiar. The day is still a little distant, and I'm facing it with the choice again to love and live for the Lord. I choose Him.

Today I begin to write this book, and my prayer is that the Holy Spirit would guide me in keeping it simple, easy-flowing, and real.

And so as you read, you will find no humongous words or theological debates to contemplate, oppose, or side with. What I write will be completely biblical, but I encourage you to test what I say. There won't be too many Bible references to put you over the top. No new "secrets" for you to ponder. Just time-tested wisdom presented in a new way . . . practical thoughts for your edification. Again, test these ideas. Try them and judge how useful they are to you.

My objective is to speak about real life for real people and to pen words of encouragement for your everyday walk with the Lord. And so, I write this for those who live their lives in real time, those who suffer and have yet to find peace. I write for the afflicted in whatever manifestation they may experience it. Whether your affliction is mental, emotional, spiritual, or physical, I write for those who, like me, would like some answers but even more need a revival of spirit.

And so, this book will be honest and straightforward—a message of hope for each of you. Be encouraged in your walk with the Lord today. You indeed can make it to the other side of whatever you are facing and be better for the experience.

This book will be written from the lessons of my own life stories; every word comes from my soul. It is the opening of my heart and the vision God gave me for my life—to be an unassuming corridor that leads to Him. To be your friend and to hold your hand tightly, to understand your brokenness, wipe your tears, be a strong shoulder, and point you to His grace, while at the same time reassuring you that God has not forgotten about you.

> *But Zion said,*
> *"The Lord has forsaken me,*
> *And the Lord has forgotten me."*
>
> *"Can a woman forget her nursing child*
> *and have no compassion on the son of her womb?*
> *Even these may forget,*
> *but I will not forget you.*
> *Behold, I have inscribed you on the palms of My hands . . ."*
> *declares the Lord.*
>
> Isaiah 49:14–16 (NASB)

A PRAYER FOR US

Before we continue, I'd like to pray for us.

Heavenly Father,
I come before you, humbled by the challenge you have placed in my
hands. Having completed this book, I give it back to you, a gift of love.
Receive my service as worship to you. Use it, Father, for your purposes
and not my own glory. Go beyond me, Master, and seed this book for
a spiritual harvest.
For every person whose hand touches this book, I ask that as they
open it they might read with expectation, looking for encouragement.
Meet them at the place of their need.
No two people will open this book with the same need or desire.
And as my words are limited, and my authority more so, I ask that your
Holy Spirit in His vastness would search every heart, scan every life,

and give these friends peace through their times of change or trouble. Give them what they truly need.

Father, some people reading this are broken. Some are lonely or depressed. Some are hanging on with the tiniest bit of faith and need you right now. So I ask that you would restore their souls and renew their strength. I ask that you would transform these unpleasant circumstances, and meanwhile grant enough strength to rise above them and grant the peace that transcends those difficulties.

Speak truth, Father, through these pages. Speak transformation. Speak renewal. Speak new life for every soul who is looking for you. Help all of us to live from here forward without bitterness—refusing cynicism, depression, or despondency—and consciously choosing joy! Cause us to learn the lessons that are life-changing.

And finally, Father, grant every person a knowing in their heart that you have not forgotten them and that you care for them more than they could ever imagine.

Thank you for hearing and answering my prayer. Thank you for being the good Father. Thank you for your undying love toward us, your children.

I ask these things according to the faith of Jesus Christ and for the sake of your kingdom alone.

Amen.

CONTENTS

1

ABOUT GOLIATH

THE GIANT WE ALL FACE

Almost everyone has heard the Bible story of David, a lowly shepherd boy, who, armed only with faith and five rocks, defeated a nine-foot-tall Philistine warrior named Goliath. The story has been woven into sermons and retold countless times. I might not have much new to add to what you already know, but indulge me for a minute as I venture down a road a little less traveled.

I'll begin my retelling of the story with Goliath taunting the army of Israel. The two armies were battling over land God had already given to the Israelites. The Philistines were intruders, and Goliath, their fiercest warrior, would stalk to the edge of the hill near their camp every morning and evening for forty days and holler across the valley at Israel's army. Defying God, Goliath essentially called himself Lord and the Israel army slaves. For the most part it was a blasphemous rant designed to taunt and torture Israel. And it did. Then, on the fortieth day, there was a turning point.

Goliath the giant *"fee, fie, foe, fummed"* his way to the cliff's edge and announced: *Choose a man from among you to come fight me. If you win (and you won't), we Philistines will be your servants. If I win (and I will, of course), all of you will become our servants.*

His challenge rang out like a death knell through the camps and terrorized all who heard it. No one came forward. In fact, the Israelites didn't even respond. No one wanted to go up against Goliath, and why would they? He was a huge, menacing villain with incredible strength. His weaponry and battle gear were massive, weighing more than the average person, it is said. Even so, Goliath was a force that needed to be reckoned with.

Now, stage left, enter David—a small, fearless shepherd boy, anointed for battle and walking with God.

The Bible doesn't give us the specifics of David's stature, but in my mind he is all of five feet tall and no more than 120 pounds, soaking wet. What we do know is the extent of his weaponry—a slingshot, which he carried at his side, and five smooth stones.

Needless to say, these two opponents were not equally matched in any sense of the word.

Still, they prepared to face each other.

Now, for me, this is where the story gets interesting. There's a battle of words, if you will. Goliath called upon his gods, and moving closer to attack David, cursed him: "Come here, and I'll give your flesh to the birds of the air and the beasts of the field!" (1 Samuel 17:44). But David was not paralyzed with fear. Instead, he ran quickly toward Goliath. Calling on the one true God, David said, "I come against you in the name of the Lord Almighty. . . . This day the Lord will hand you over to me, and I'll strike you down and cut off your head" (1 Samuel 17:45–46).

Picture that.

What I wouldn't give to have the kind of faith that when put directly in the path of a deadly giant would be all I needed.

Once David spoke those words, the battle was over. You see, words have power. Whether we realize it or not, our words are constantly creating either positive or negative influences in our lives. Proverbs 18:21 tells us that the tongue has the power of life and death. So even everyday speaking, done as effortlessly as we breathe, is actually helping to shape our future, for good or bad (more on this in a later chapter).

What's important to note here is that David shaped the outcome of the battle with his words. He spoke victory. And after weeks of Goliath's taunting and threats, in a confrontation that lasted mere minutes, David flung a stone that hit Goliath squarely between the eyes. Goliath fell, and David beheaded him with Goliath's own sword. Israel won, and David went on to become king.

Over the years this story has become *the* banner of encouragement when we face seemingly insurmountable obstacles. Sunday school writings and even political speeches tell us that anyone can be a modern-day David and overcome their Goliath. And we believe it. We believe it because we want to believe in the underdog. We want to cheer for him, pray for him, and favor him. In fact, we imagine that we *are* David, gathering all the faith we can muster, collecting our stones, rearing back, and aiming to stop all that hinders our progress.

Because of the example of David's victory, we have a basis for hope.

But what if Goliath had not fallen? Would David have been called a man of lesser faith?

What if Goliath and David were the same physical size? Would the story be less inspiring?

What if the battle raged for hours with no obvious winner? Would God be any less sovereign?

The answers: no, no, and most emphatically NO.

You see, I believe the story of David and Goliath is more than a story about having faith to triumph over the giant that opposes us. Rather, it illustrates that life itself is the giant we face. I contend that on a deeper level, and despite the appearance of duality, Goliath does not represent individual life challenges or opposition, but all of them combined.

For life is all at once a huge and masterful journey filled with delightful things as well as things that break our hearts. It is a combination of molehills and towering mountains that seem to grow out of nowhere. One day we are just minding our business, going about our daily tasks; and the next we come face-to-face with overwhelming problems, obstacles, or needs. One minute we are playing with our children and watching them grow, and in the next we are calling for an Amber Alert trying to find them.

Indeed, life is a huge and unpredictable ride. But I don't have to tell you that—you know your Goliath. You recognize his walk and the thunder of his voice. You smell his breath, and you stand paralyzed before his taunts—via the bills you can't pay, the mail you can't bring yourself to open, the people you can't please, the job you can't find, the relationships you can't fix, the habits you can't break, the failures you can't forget, the future that looks grim.

These super-sized challenges have swaggered and strutted into our lives, stolen our sleep, embezzled our peace, and robbed our joy for what seems to be a lifetime. We have been silenced by fear while they've remained arrogant, menacing, deadly, and seemingly impossible to defeat.

But take heart, my friends. Be of good cheer, for victory over what really threatens has already come—at the cross. "In this world you will have trouble," Jesus tells us. "But take heart! I have overcome the world" (John 16:33 NIV). Long before we walk onto any battlefield to confront the enemy that opposes *our* lives, know that our enemy is also the enemy of God. And though that enemy wants to rob us of our joy, our inheritance in Jesus Christ, our hope for eternity, he has been defeated by God. Christ has overcome him!

————

About a year ago, I visited a children's hospital solely to encourage families through their hard times. As I was passing through the corridors, following the lead of the Holy Spirit, I was drawn by what I call a light. I looked into a room and will never forget the bald, pale child with the beautiful smile, propped up in her bed and motioning me in. For the sake of her privacy, I'll call her Amy.

Amy was busy coloring and labeling small cards.

"What are you coloring?" I asked.

"It's my birthday in two weeks," she replied. "I'm going to invite all my friends to celebrate."

Amy's mom sat next to her bed and was coloring as well. She smiled gently and politely passed me several cards, turning a list of names so I could view them.

"Well, how old will you be, Miss Amy?" I asked.

"Eight," she answered, as she tilted her head to the side and colored. Then she started talking, and oh boy, did she talk. I have no idea how I kept up with the torrent of words that flowed from that child. Mom smiled at me while I made faces that hinted at what I was thinking: *Wow! Little girls are expressive.*

It wasn't too long, though, before Amy began to tire. Mom pulled the cards away from her and promised that she and I would finish them. Then, as Amy lay back to rest, Mom explained why Amy had been hospitalized.

About a year earlier, she had been diagnosed with leukemia. She began a very aggressive treatment to move the cancer into remission. Chemotherapy had caused hair loss, upset stomach, weight gain, fevers, sore back (from spinal taps), skin rash, shortness of breath, blood in the urine, vomiting; the list went on.

Amy was in pain much of the time, but she was a trooper, her mom said. A few months before my visit, Amy had surgery to place a Port-a-Cath into a large vessel near her heart.

"The port is infected and has to be replaced," Amy interjected. "But God is good."

I couldn't believe what I'd just heard. I turned to look at her and to find an understanding of how such faith was possible in such a young child.

Quickly her mom added, "All the time."

Mom and I colored in what was an amazingly comfortable silence. When we finished the cards, we exchanged phone numbers, and I said a prayer for Amy before I left.

A week later I mailed Amy a birthday gift, and shortly after that her mom called me. She said Amy got the gift and had her party, but then passed away two days after her eighth birthday. Through tears, I offered my condolences. Mom ended the call by reminding me that God is good.

In my view, Amy's life mirrored David's. She too fought the good fight of faith. She too stood against the giant and won. Not in the same way as David, but in knowing that the promises of God are eternal and therefore not reliant upon the outcome of our earthly battles. Real victory is in the everlasting.

We won't always have the spectacular results we want in life. Sometime our stories will be heart-shattering, like Amy's. We won't always save the world, our nation, our family, or even our sanity. But whether God chose to intercede that day to defeat Goliath or it was David that lay dead in the field, God is no less sovereign.

Whether Amy went into remission or went home to be with the Lord, God is no less compassionate, and He is indeed good.

And whether He heals you today or in eternity, God is God, above all.

Our struggles are not about right or wrong, win or lose, can or cannot—they are often just life as it is. And when life saunters about with its thundering voice, determined to be lord over our souls and make us slaves to its whims, perhaps a second look will reveal that life itself is really not so big at all.

2

LIFE KEEPS HAPPENING

AND THE PEACE OF GOD . . .

What is big to you can only be determined by you.

Experiences, challenges, and even relationships are all perceived on different levels. What might first appear to be "big" or negative can later be viewed on a deeper level as positive—something that will lead to growth, greater awareness, compassion, or even peace.

You see, there is a polarity to life, and within its giant framework—where we find the ups and downs, the ins and outs, the good, bad, and everything in the middle—we determine our response to life. We draw our conclusions and lines in the sand.

It's our choice to embrace an all-encompassing life right now, complete with its wonderful diversity of events and possibilities, or live life by the numbers, fighting against the "now" and looking to connect the dots we hope will lead to future contentment.

Personally, I am choosing to live the all-encompassing and aim toward complete surrender and joy. Although some of life's lessons for me need to be learned and then relearned, every day I'm making a conscious decision not to sweat the small stuff.

I believe that is what James is talking about when he suggests that we "count it *all* joy, my brothers, when you meet trials of various kinds" (James 1:2 esv, emphasis added). Consider every detail, every situation, and every life challenge a blessing, for this is what gives us the confidence to live life without struggling.

Easier said than done, you say? Not really. You see, all that life is, it will be—with or without our permission or active participation. To struggle with the "what-ifs," "why-me's," and the "who, what, and when" is futile. It's like an insect struggling in a spider web, intensifying the call to the spider, or flailing your arms when you're drowning, or pushing against a python, causing the snake to tighten its grip. I'd much rather muddle through life with the peace of God than struggle against it—period.

Just last week I was balancing my checkbook. I hadn't been on the road for a while, and without steady income, plus covering my son's college expenses, my finances were short for the month. My first response was panic and sadness.

The panic came because I've been homeless and hungry before— in the not so distant past, in fact. And the last thing I ever want to be is homeless or hungry again. Although my heart knows and trusts what God says, my flesh still thinks His promises need my help.

To be perfectly honest, there have been times when I felt little hope for happiness. At one point, I was up to my neck in so many bills I hated to see the mailman coming. There was a place on my dining room table where I kept mail I had no intention of opening because there was never anything good inside. There have been times when I was afraid or confused and even times when I felt so lonely for a husband that it was easier to close myself off.

But that was then. Today, the Holy Spirit reminds me that God will supply all of my needs according to His riches in glory by Christ Jesus (see Philippians 4:19).

Then He guides me to Philippians 4:11–12, where Paul says, "Not that I speak from want, for I have learned to be content in whatever circumstances I am. I know how to get along with humble means, and I also know how to live in prosperity; in any and every circumstance I have learned the secret of being filled and going hungry, both of having abundance and suffering need" (NASB).

And then the Holy Spirit reminds me of Moses, who didn't see the Promised Land from this side; Mother Teresa, who suffered from depression; and numerous others who have dealt with alcohol abuse, broken marriages, and other challenges, too many to mention.

And finally, the Holy Spirit gives me understanding. It is this: I don't think the apostle Paul (in Philippians 4:11–12) was talking about being content with the simple variations of life circumstances, but rather a state of mind. I think he is telling us he had learned to live in humble acceptance of the "now." Whether "now" was a mansion or a homeless shelter, food or hunger, freedom or imprisonment, his spiritual well-being was unchanged by what was happening around him.

Let's not rush past this. In fact, let me say it again. Paul counsels us that our situations in life are what they are. Fighting them is futile. Being truly prosperous—defined by our spiritual wellness and state of mind—is a gift to be found in every circumstance. Prosperity is not an outward condition but an inward determination.

Bravo, Paul! I like that. And perhaps for me that means I will never get far enough ahead of my monthly expenses to again buy Chanel, but my needs will be met and I will be content. I might remain single, but I am enjoying the intrigue of waiting for a husband who may or may not come. I am opening the mail again, and though I am still finding bills, I am also finding coupons, notices about improved credit, and nice letters from readers.

My cousin Ronnie and I maintain a very close friendship. I talk a lot and he listens. Sometimes he'll respond to my questions by simply saying, "All is well." That's cool talk, and it means "Despite any possible doubt, everything's cool." He says the same thing after I've apologized for talking and questioning so much.

That's my word for you today: Despite any possible doubt, everything is cool.

Are there any easy solutions? Frankly, no, but every situation will mean something a little different for each of us—depending on our perspective. After all, this is a personal journey we're on.

As for me, all the unpredictability in life is what makes the journey so rich and so much fun. Sometimes life is hard. Most of the time life will catch us off guard, but life is always good. What more can we ask for? What more should we expect?

My one bit of advice for you now is to embrace all of life with joyful optimism, relishing every moment of it! Understanding, of course, that in the end what matters is not the number of breaths we take in a moment. What ultimately matters is the number of moments that take our breath away. These yield gifts of confidence and humility that lead to a "knowing in our knowers," as my grandmother used to say, that all is truly well! And it *is*, you know!

3

THE OVERWHELMING THINGS OF EVERY DAY

MORE THAN YOU CAN BEAR

Lately, as the usual headlines about local crime and national catastrophes give way to global human interest stories, I've been reading and watching the news with a lot more compassion than before.

Stories about ordinary people suffering through extraordinary circumstances fill the pages. As financial losses force our neighbors to sacrifice much-needed medications to keep the lights on in their homes, some of our seniors go hungry in order to pay a mortgage or rent that falls farther and farther behind. There are challenges in our government, there is dissension among religious leaders, and there is brokenness in many homes.

It is heartbreaking to see many we know suffer opposition and struggle to persevere.

As believers, we seek to remain faithful even while we may

scramble to make ends meet through a failing economy, suffer deteriorating health, know job loss, and have family members with addictions, moral failure, or other difficult circumstances or situations. All these things make even the simplest task weigh heavy on our shoulders. Sometimes twenty-four hours in a day doesn't seem like enough, and that little voice inside our heads won't stop and allow us to sleep. Life can change faster than we can acclimate to it, but we are comforted in knowing that God is in control and that He will not allow us to be tested beyond what we can bear (see 1 Corinthians 10:13). *Right?*

Well, brace yourself, because I believe God will not only allow us to experience more than we could normally bear on our own but He will also on occasion purpose backbreaking burdens for us to carry and heat intense enough to transform us.

Just as God allowed Job, John the Baptist, and many other faithful believers to be tested and troubled beyond their *human strength*, He may test us. Even the apostle Paul was sorely tested. In 2 Corinthians 1:8–9, Paul listed some of them: "We think you ought to know, dear brothers and sisters, about the trouble we went through in the province of Asia. We were crushed and overwhelmed beyond our ability to endure, and we thought we would never live through it. In fact, we expected to die" (NLT).

Surely we've all been there. Surely we've known pain intense enough to stop a beating heart and anguish deep enough to rob us of our vocabulary. Sometimes crisis points exist on so many levels that life becomes almost unbearable. Sometimes there is so much going on in our lives that we tire of persevering. Sometimes life breaks our heart.

But thank God, He declares that He is close to the brokenhearted and rescues those whose spirits are crushed (Psalm 34:18 NLT). He heals the brokenhearted and bandages their wounds (Psalm

147:3 NLT). In our weakness, God says His grace is all we need. His power works best in weakness (2 Corinthians 12:9 NLT).

———

Before a speaking engagement some time ago, I had dinner with a woman from the host church. I'll call her Betty.

Betty and I enjoyed pleasant dinner conversation, and I found her to be an amazing woman, full of encouragement and love for the Lord. Toward the end of the meal, I asked, "If you could ask God for anything and get it within minutes, what would it be?"

Without hesitation, Betty responded, "I'd ask Him for real, honest-to-goodness rest." I watched her tightly twist her paper napkin as she went on to explain her statement. Her eyes watered and her bottom lip quivered as she told me how a few years earlier, while she was in the middle of a divorce, her sister found their father's body in his bed after he committed suicide.

Betty said her father did not believe in God at the time of his death, and while she knew she should leave God-things to God, she could not settle the deep restlessness and pain in her heart. She had searched the Scriptures, called on the name of the Lord for deliverance, and fasted for God to give her peace about her dad. But rest had not come.

Betty was crying when she finally said, "My church family keeps telling me to be faithful, that God is in control in spite of what I see, that I need to trust God, that some things are the result of sin in the world and that God is letting it have its course, but how do I let it go?"

I think Betty represents many of us today. Though what her church told her is all true, these answers do not always bring comfort, because pain sometimes overrides our faith. Consequently, we look for God to explain things so that we can accept a situation and find comfort rather than in the way He has already taught us: by our letting go.

How do you let go, you ask? Consider this: At any moment, life is exactly the way it is. You are the way you are, the people in your life are exactly the way they are, and your circumstance is what it is. This is true whether you like it or not. But when you accept the truth—without replacing any part of it with your own ideals—you let go. You let go when you don't try to arrange or control all the outcomes or others' actions. Letting go is accepting life in all its diversity without fighting against it.

So breathe.

This, my friend, is perhaps the one lesson I have learned umpteen times today and will need to learn again tomorrow. You see, in Leslieland, where troubles are put down for a while and picked up again with the rationalization that perhaps they are God's will, I need to apply this lesson each time.

Like right now, for example.

Two years ago I bought a used SUV for a good price and a better reason. I live in the mountains, and winters here can be brutal. Well, over the summer the car started to ride a little rocky, and unusual noises were coming from under the hood. The short story: The transmission went out. But by God's grace it was under warranty, so the car was repaired without cost to me.

A few months later, two and a half to be exact, the car started riding rough again. As suspected, it was the transmission—again . . . and the water pump, and the rear wheel bearings, and the tires, and the antilock-brake system. All to the tune of too-much-to-sink-into-a-car-with-an-expired-warranty. So I did what I thought best: I took the money I would have spent on repairs and bought a brand-new car. It was great for exactly two weeks.

Last night my son, Eliot, was driving the new car to go play basketball, when he hit a deep pothole and blew out a tire. He put on the spare and came right home.

This morning I got an early start. I had a lot to do, so I took my brand-new car—still with the new-car smell—to the dealership to get a new tire put on. Simple, right?

Well, not so much.

After examining the car, the mechanic concluded that the pothole Eliot hit must have been huge. So huge, it not only punctured the tire, it bent the rim. Both needed to be replaced. And neither was covered by warranty or insurance. I had to pay full price. Then, since the tire was not in stock, one needed to be ordered and would be delivered in four hours, and I needed to pick up my dog, Max, in three and take a phone meeting with my editor in two. And to add insult to injury, I hadn't even had a decent cup of coffee.

Needless to say, I spent the entire morning in a classic Leslie mood, and by early afternoon, I was over the top. I was tired of waiting, cranky, and annoyed with the entire world. By two o'clock, when the replacement tire still hadn't arrived, I got that little knot of frustration in my gut and could have cried.

And then the God of the eleventh hour, the Father of compassion and God of all comfort, who comforts us in *all* our troubles, found me—sitting smack dab in the middle of relearning the very lesson this chapter is about. How poetic is God?

You see, I'm now even more sure that He doesn't deal with all of us in the same way. Some may very well endure backbreaking burdens—like James, who was persecuted and put to death at the order of Herod (Acts 12:1–2), or Betty, who lives with the pain of her father's suicide. Others will struggle with the things of every day that can overwhelm, like trying to quit smoking or getting a car fixed.

Peter tells us not to be surprised when bad things happen,

because they *do* happen . . . they are a part of life. And while in this life there is trouble, there is also *comfort*. There may be suffering, but there is also *comfort*. There may be distress and hardships and things we don't understand, but there is always *comfort*. For in all of life's difficulties and troubles, God's grace and comfort will be equal to our need even in the everyday things. And in all things His grace will sustain us.

Sitting here in this car dealership, I could easily continue to stew in all the could-haves and should-haves, but to what end? Will my frustrations move time forward? Will my anger move it back? I can spiritualize and conjure up some gripping revelation from the Lord, but for what point? There are no new lessons to be learned from this situation except the one I've learned before. What I'm experiencing now is just life—being lived—and it is what it is. I choose to let go.

Besides, even if the Lord does allow for a particular trial to finish us off, separation from this world is not the end of life. For believers, it is the beginning! And that should be our focus through it all, our unending life in the presence of God—happy, holy, and healthy forever!

What have I come to learn about life here on earth? Today I know no other answer than this, and we can count on it: Life is . . . exactly what it is. Let go!

4

SPENT

WHEN YOU'VE GOT NO MORE TEARS

Despite our best efforts to leave things to God, it's easy to get down when difficult times don't improve. What happens after you stand steadfast on God's Word, depend on Him for strength, and wait for Him to resolve things to your expectations, and you still reach the point where you have cried what seems a lifetime of tears?

What do you do when there's nothing left in you to persevere?

I remember seeing a quote from Frankin Roosevelt: "When you get to the end of your rope, tie a knot and hang on." My advice? Forget the knot—it takes too long—grab hold with both hands! When a situation reaches this intensity, don't waste time looking for some way around it. You must go through it.

Consider this. Life is huge, and as discussed in the previous chapter, most everything has positive and negative aspects. Therefore, no single challenge will have one simple and straightforward answer. Life is far too complex.

And then there is God. He does not do things as we would or think how we think, thus providing one-dimensional or linear answers to our questions. That's too limited. Instead, He considers all things (Romans 8:28) and causes them to work together to bring about His perfect work in us and through our lives. He does not provide us with answers. He assigns meaning. For example, a particular incident might appear to be isolated and critical for only one person, but with a closer look, and an open heart, its spiritual meaning and how it is part of God's redemptive plan will be revealed.

Sometimes this revelation is only possible in hindsight. That was my experience with David. Our first conversation flowed easily, as if I'd known him all my life. He was a consultant on a project I had at work. We spoke often those first few days. I enjoyed working with him. He was delightful in spirit and a self-described optimist who always looked for the brighter side and the good in people. I appreciated that about him. He never missed an opportunity to encourage someone to stay strong, to never give up, to never stop loving . . . or dancing.

So it came as quite a shock when one day, by way of an e-mail sent to everyone on an Internet forum, the news came that the dancing had stopped. The e-mail's subject line read:

Prelude to a Suicide: I'm Dead

In what followed, David revealed how severe financial and health problems had brought him to the point of wanting to end his life. He wrote about past hurts, sinking into poverty, going hungry, and just being exhausted by his private battle. He talked about lessons he wanted to leave us: to love our families, to enjoy the outdoors, to talk with friends, to hug our kids.

David's suicide note stopped my heart and thousands more across America.

When I finally got through to the police department in David's area, I could hear officers in the background taking calls from others desperate to save the life of a not-so-ordinary man.

I hung up the phone and prayed.

Thankfully, David was rescued by police officers and taken to a hospital, where the switchboard there experienced the same volume of calls as the police had earlier. People from all over came together to support David—to be the outstretched hands of God.

And that's the idea of it. Even if you can't see God at a crisis point, know that He works by His Spirit and through His Word to accomplish His purposes in our lives. He is always moving the pieces around in order that some might be saved and come to know Him. That's what it's all about, really . . . the salvation of the world!

On the surface, David's low point is tragic. But on a deeper level, it is a beautiful story about a love that goes beyond the physical: God's love. It's a story about grace that is richer than silver and gold: God's grace. It speaks of mercy and hope that reaches into even the darkest night of a soul to deliver light: God's light. And the message therein can only be found in the richness of His glory! *Selah.*

Through God's love, grace, and light, David did recover, helped by his online network of friends who rallied around him and helped him get a fresh start.

Some might be satisfied with ending David's story here. But remembering that God doesn't give answers, He gives meaning, this, to me, is where David's story begins.

Let's suppose that God's purpose in all of this extended beyond just one person. And let's suppose that God really is bigger than the boundaries of time. That means that before time, God, as the Master Networker, purposed to gather thousands of people who, as part of a redemptive plan, would respond to David's life-or-death situation, all to bear witness to God's extensive reach and to save the life of one man.

I believe in a God like that! I believe God used thousands of people to minister to David's pain, and He used David's pain to minister to the needs of thousands. I believe God intentionally connects us to one another, using relationships to strengthen, support, and deliver His comfort in order to achieve His goal.

And so, we really are our brother's keeper, responsible to one another for our actions and the consequences that will result, responsible to God for things that relate to our spiritual wholeness, and responsible to ourselves in making sure our lives embrace God's decided meaning.

In nature, the grapevine is a perfect example of connection. Its branches intertwine to the extent that it is hard to tell where one branch begins and another one ends. This intertwining supports the entire vine, helping to strengthen it against wind and rain. Each branch braces the other, helping each to stay connected to the vine.

The Bible says God is the vine and we are the branches (John 15:5). Our connection, both to Christ and to one another, is essential to living as God has planned. Each of us are meant to support each other, bracing through the tough times in life, encouraging through change, being the voice of hope through doubt, all while holding on to the vine.

We should pay attention to one another and share love in necessary ways: clean houses, cook, do laundry, and listen. Pray, hope, help to brace each other for the next invariable storm, and listen some more. In times when we feel strongest, we should give ourselves to be vessels of support, knowing that our lives are tenu-ous, our existence indeed delicate and so temporary that we *must* take the time to connect and show love.

And when, like my friend David, you are at your wit's end, be encouraged that there is a much greater purpose to personal heartbreak than a broken heart! God can and will redeem your situation with His meaning if you let Him. And then the ultimate blessings—peace of mind, peace in your home, and peace throughout your life—will be yours!

5

SOMETIMES WE FALL

THEN ALL THE KING'S HORSES . . .

Everyone experiences challenges in life. And while some people march through valiantly and seemingly unscathed, others go kicking and screaming. Still, we all do our best to endure. Over the past few years, however, I have come to believe that it isn't as important *how* we go through, but that we *get* through.

As we have touched on, sometimes God doesn't want to change our *situation,* He wants to change *us.*

When I was a little girl, I loved the story of Humpty Dumpty. It was one of my favorite nursery rhymes. For some reason I got a kick out of visualizing a huge egg falling off a wall, breaking into a thousand pieces; but in my mind he was still smiling. And even though "all the king's horses and all the king's men couldn't put Humpty together again," my little hands would start clapping from the sheer excitement of it all.

From a grown-up perspective, though, Humpty Dumpty's story loses its fascination. It too closely resembles real life.

Many of us teeter between being faithful and backpedaling—guessing about God and grasping at straws for what ails us. When our problems outweigh the sum of our solutions, we struggle and wobble and try our best to hold on until finally we reach the point that unless the King himself intervenes, our souls will shatter and our lives will break.

But what if the King's goal is not to keep us in our current condition but to transform us? What if every hardship we face is but one aspect of a much bigger picture that is intended to help us lose faith in the temporal and pursue a deeper knowledge of God and share in His holiness? (See Philippians 3:10; Hebrews 12:10.)

What if the King's desire is not to send angels or friends to help put our same old lives back together again, but to himself make something beautiful from the pieces of our lives? What if God's purpose for us through our pain is not a temporal fix but an inner transformation?

Consider the butterfly. Starting as a caterpillar, it undergoes a metamorphosis in its cocoon in which it is completely transformed. The process is comprehensive and intensive, and eventually the butterfly breaks free of the cocoon and emerges as a beautiful new creation.

So I believe it is with each of us. As we break free from religious traditions that stray from the Word of God, we come into the knowledge of truth. God helps us transcend old behavior patterns—tempers, attitudes, misunderstandings—and fight our way out of the hard shell and into a new life.

Some years ago, when I began my transformation—the renewing of my mind—I thought, *Great! I'll walk upright before God, and He'll bless me for it. Things will be so much better.* And they were, but not in the sense of living a fairy tale. Rather, I found peace in the process of surrendering attitudes and behaviors that had been central to my usual responses to life.

Initially, it was difficult to see myself under the bright light of His truth. But as I gave myself over to the change, I set aside all the moving pieces in life and became wrapped up in the stillness of His presence. I quieted the static sounds of confusion and became a better listener to the creative noise of life and to the voice of God. As I yielded myself to the pain of inner change, my heart skipped a beat and began pounding in rhythm with the Holy Spirit of God.

With an understanding that God's ways are not our ways, I stopped trying to bypass the tough life for the conventional and began to embrace the hiddenness, or mystery, of His ways.

When we are transformed, what emerges are new eyes designed for a Christ-fixed focus today, tomorrow, and forever; lips shaped for singing His praise even when storms come; ears tuned to hear the voice of God; and a heart of obedience that responds as the mother of Jesus did: Father, through it all, "may it be to me as you have said" (Luke 1:38).

And though I cannot verbally explain exactly what happens inside us, I am convinced God did not design our transformation so that we could make it through the next "thing" but rather to strengthen us so that we could make it through this entire thing called life!

And that feels good. It tastes good. It makes me know that God is fully engaged in our lives.

That's all we really long for, isn't it? A sense of being important to God, knowing we are significant enough to get His attention? We want His presence and assurance from Him that our lives aren't lost in the crowd or in the barrage of prayers directed toward Him.

Don't we just want some confidence deep in our souls that God isn't so busy with the perils of this world that we have become a bother to Him and He has forgotten to look in on us? Not necessarily to soften a fall, but prepare us for the road ahead—just in case?

That's the thing with falls of every kind. Whether it's hitting the street on an icy walkway, slipping on wet pavement, tripping over toys, or stumbling over our own feet, each of these moments usually come when we are going our merry way, totally unprepared and paying little attention to what's ahead. Then down we go.

I, for one, am particularly thrown off by inanimate objects. In fact, the other night the top step of an escalator reached up to greet me.

I was on my way to San Diego to lead a weekend women's retreat. About four hours into my travel, I was beginning to tire just a bit. The first leg of my flight had been delayed out of New York's Stewart Airport, and the connection in Atlanta was on time and at the gate. Translation: Run!

Usually I'm pretty smart in my travel attire. Loose-fitting clothes and comfortable shoes meet the occasional requirements of sprints and hurdles. That day, however, was not one of those days. At 85 muggy degrees, a summer dress and flip-flops was my outfit of choice.

I rushed through the airport. Gate C5 was in the next terminal and about halfway down the row of gates. Being an all-efficient travelista, I decided on the way that I should confirm my car service in San Diego.

Picture this: I was rushing along, holding my cell phone with my right hand, carrying my laptop and purse with my left hand, and screaming my name into the phone while looking for Gate C5. I was sure they must have been making the final boarding call.

My mind raced faster than my feet as I ran up an escalator. *Pause from the story.*

Now, everyone knows the last step on the escalator is a bit tricky; you have to make a little jump and then quickly move your feet forward to catch up with the speed of your body, right?

Resume story.

I was rushing past the "now" moment I was in—anticipating the moment the plane would take off and wondering why the reservation agent at the car service couldn't hear me—when I caught sight of the last step sliding under the floor. I did the "jump" thing all right, but down I went!

I forgot to move my feet forward.

I'll spare you all the ugly details of the flying purse, the airborne hem of my dress, the cell phone, one flip-flop, and the only bit of ego I had left. What I will say is that if you ever get the opportunity to look at the ceiling in an airport, don't do it. You'll be surprised at what you see.

Anyway, a nice man helped me up and gathered most of my things. I'm not sure if I was more embarrassed by the fall or by what had spilled from my purse. I left most of it behind from the sheer horror of ownership.

I boarded the plane physically disheveled, mentally scattered, and in the nick of time. Soon after takeoff, the lady next to me confessed she had witnessed my fall from "grace-full." She smiled with me and shared a few of her most embarrassing moments. She was a kind soul.

Later that night, in the stillness of my hotel room, I tossed and turned, replaying the sound of impact and inventory of the faces that had witnessed it. Finally, I told the Lord about it. Still reeling from humiliation, I said, "Father, you are my Redeemer and you make all things new. What can you make of me?"

In the gentle way in which I have learned to depend on, the Lord reminded me that I have carried around things a lot more embarrassing than what was in my purse. I've carried greed, ego, and anger. I've held on to resentment, envy, lust, and pride. And although I've done my best to keep a Christ-fixed focus in my journey, I've worried so much about what's ahead that I've not taken notice of today's grace.

Still, God *is* our Redeemer, and He will uphold us in our time of trouble. He is loving and gentle and there for us, always, even in life's most embarrassing and ungraceful moments. And that's good news because, let's face it, we're all just human and sometimes we fall.

6

GOD IS NO LESS GOOD

EVEN IN THE DARK!

Life today is all about change. We're moving faster in every direction, and right now both as a nation and individually we're facing one of the most difficult periods in recent history. As a result, the market is flooded with self-help books and "secrets" about laws of the universe—all supposedly to help us better adjust to these changing times.

But not only are we living through changing situations, we're living with inconsistency.

One day society tells us to think positively and everything will follow accordingly. Next we're told to "call forth" the things we want and a richer life will result. One idea, and then another, claims to be the latest and greatest, entangling us more and more in societal rhetoric and less and less in truth.

The truth is, as we try to deal with the highs and lows of a changing world, society will always offer us "solutions" that are contrary to the Word of God.

However, our sovereign God—the Supreme Authority—does not change. He is the only way to a truly richer life. He is not subject to any power or law we devise. He is not shaped by our ups and downs. He does not follow any "law of correspondence," nor will His character or Word ever be outweighed on a false doctrinal scale. He is the same God who made the world, the same God who saved Noah, the same God who gave the Law through Moses, who appointed David king, who spoke through the prophets; the same God who has revealed himself to us through Jesus Christ. Our varying life conditions can never change this truth.

A simple illustration: Recently I was on a perfect date, with the perfect man, at the perfect restaurant, having the perfect meal over the most perfect conversation. When the waiter came to refill my coffee, his arm brushed against my water glass and knocked it over in my lap. Of course I was a little more than stunned.

Imagine sitting in a cozy warm seat and then suddenly being doused with ice-cold water. I almost jumped through the roof.

And while I did not celebrate this incident, I did immediately understand that it was just an accident. And so all things considered, the little mishap, though unfortunate, took nothing away from the evening. I was still on the perfect date, with the perfect man, at the perfect restaurant, having the perfect meal over the most perfect conversation. I was just now doing it in a wet skirt. Hmmm. Go figure.

You see, I believe the adage that life is 10 percent what happens to us and 90 percent how we respond to it. And the goodness of our lives is not determined by what life brings to us, but by the attitude we bring to life.

This is how I see God. His goodness is not determined by

our varying circumstances—how much money is in the bank, the house we live in, or even our credentials. His love is not greater at any one time or another. In our sickness and in our health, God is God. Whether we feast or go hungry, God is good. In a mansion or on the street, He reigns. In circumstances of want or of plenty, God's mercy is forever.

I realize, of course, it can be challenging to push past a hungry belly or a restless night to acknowledge God's goodness and His steadfast character. I know that loosening the grip of fear and trusting Him for light when disconnection notices loom overhead is almost impossible. And I agree that sometimes just knowing of God's goodness is not enough.

You see, His goodness will only give us peace when we couple it with the knowledge of His promises and an understanding of His sovereignty.

Let me explain. The sovereignty of God is not so simple as to be only about His having the freedom to do exactly as He desires. God's actions are reflective of His nature, and He will never do anything contradictory to His nature.

Because God is righteous, just, and fair, He will never do anything that is unrighteous, unjust, or unfair. Because He is truth and is holy and compassionate, He will never lie, never agree with our sin, and never minimize our troubles. His actions are motivated by a love that is as He is—always perfect, always full, always complete, always unchangeable, and always, always, always there for us! (Malachi 3:6; 2 John 1:1–3; John 17:24; Romans 5:5–10)

———

A few years ago, I was called to a home in the city of Newburgh, New York, where a single mother of three was facing intense trials. Laid off from her job, she was finding it hard to make ends even wave at each other, let alone meet. I was told she had little food and her electricity had been turned off.

Her daughter, about thirteen years old, greeted me at the front door with a warm smile. "My mother is in her prayer closet right now," she explained. "But come in, she's almost finished."

I sat on the sofa, and my soul was quickly touched by what I saw and felt in that home. From a room somewhere in the back, I could hear the mother singing short songs in Spanish. I didn't understand a word, but I knew she was praising God. The children were laughing quietly with each other as they held flashlights over a board game. They played on the floor in a beautiful peace.

Being the emotional person I am, it took little time before I was in tears and giving silent praises to God. The love in that home—not just love for God but for one another—was humbling.

When Mom entered the room, her hands were slightly lifted as she said, "*Dios es aún bueno en la oscuridad.*" She greeted me with the same smile as her daughter had. I explained who I was and that I had brought funds to help her out. She hugged me and told me she had been expecting me.

I didn't even have to ask, because I know God. I knew in my spirit that the Holy Spirit had comforted her in knowing that she had a friend in high places, and that He would, as He promises, take care of her needs according to His riches in Christ Jesus (Philippians 4:19).

James expressed it this way: "Every good and perfect gift is from above, coming down from the Father of the heavenly lights, who does not change like shifting shadows" (James 1:17 NIV).

You see, it makes no difference whether the lights are on or off. God is still a Comforter, a Peace-Giver, a loving Father, and a Friend—even in the dark.

In a world where consistency is a rare commodity—where public opinion changes with the wind, where life goes from good to mundane to trying to catch our breath while chasing our tails—we have to remember that only God stands above it all. It is His truth that deepens us, strengthens us, and gives us hope for our journey. In His promises we find the lessons that grow our churches and raise our children to be disciples of the King. When all hope seems lost, God remains consistent and true to His Word: "My kindness shall not depart from you" (Isaiah 54:10 NKJV).

God is the light that banishes darkness. Yet the dark moments are the ones we learn the most from and recount from generation to generation. These are the times that give us the understanding of how infinitely rich life is. For only in struggle do we recognize the simple beauty in life—the art of a sovereign God: the laughter of playing children, the night sky alive with stars, the fresh smell of grass at morning dew, the warm yellow autumn moon, early birds in song, the first smile after you've fallen in love, trees that go on forever in every color and shape, the smell of the air after it rains, the rushing great rivers and lakes, and puppy breath.

And so in the light of all God has done and all He is, yes, my friend, I do agree: *Dios es aún bueno en la oscuridad!* God is good, even in the dark!

7

THE DISTANCE BETWEEN US

GOD, CAN YOU HEAR ME?

Some years ago, when I began my first study of the book of Romans, I was excited to learn more about Paul's masterpiece on grace, as some call it. By the end of the study, I had collected so much from Romans I began calling it my little book of jewels.

The eighth chapter of Romans is my favorite, but one passage in particular became my theme song: "I am persuaded that neither death nor life, nor angels nor principalities nor powers, nor things present nor things to come, nor height nor depth, nor any other created thing, shall be able to separate us from the love of God which is in Christ Jesus our Lord" (vv. 38–39 NKJV).

I know my relationship with God. I know how much I love Him, how much I like Him, and how very much I enjoy being with Him. I love the ability to be myself and relax with Him, to laugh, cry, and even joke with Him about things like someday seeing Him and passing out from the sheer excitement of it all. He is real to me, and it's important that my life is pleasing in His sight.

When we are together, I'm like a little girl with her father, riding her bicycle with no hands and shouting, "Daddy, look at me . . . look . . . look at me, Daddy!"

Normally I imagine the Lord waving at me with His huge arms in the air, smiling and saying, "Yes, baby, I see you." But a few months ago, it wasn't that way at all. I was just riding. And "just riding" was taking all my energy. I wasn't sure I wanted Daddy to see me like that.

Don't misunderstand me. I knew in my head that He did see me. I knew in my head that when I called out I already had His complete attention. He is a good Father. But for some reason my heart felt almost grieved—detached, like I had nothing left to my faith. I could have written Paul's declaration about God's love a hundred times on a blackboard and it still would not have penetrated my thick heart. I was in a weird place, and the silence there was deafening.

There was a longing in my belly for God that I couldn't quite satisfy. And even in my want to be near to Him, I felt distant from Him, not motivated and wondering why. I kept singing that song "Lord, Light the Fire Again," but there were no sparks. I sought answers in the Word of God, but my Bible felt like it weighed a ton. I would pick it up and be exhausted. Some nights I couldn't find the energy to get on my knees to pray, so I didn't.

I went to church and cried through sermons. I went to the church altar for prayer. I felt empty in my giving. I tried talking it through with my sister. I know this might sound silly, but I was afraid I was losing the best relationship I'd ever had, which saddened me most of all.

One day I wrote this:

God was quiet again today. Note to self: Listen more.

God was distant again last night. Note to Leslie: Where are you?

God was walking through the valley. I saw Him there.

About two months into this period, I got an e-mail from my friend and editor, Jeff. Not knowing what I was going through, he wanted to share an article with me. Entitled "Watch God," it talked about feeling disconnected from God and revealed how Mother Teresa had felt a "complete absence of God's presence" for nearly fifty years. This experience was described as a "dark night of the soul," a phrase coined by St. John of the Cross.

The dark night of the soul is the lonely, painful process Christians sometimes go through when we don't "feel" our faith. We feel distant from God. We question ourselves and challenge Him. But as we endure more internal suffering, this feeling of absence can become a positive thing. It works to separate us from the desires of the world, making us more able to accomplish the purposes for which Christ has called us. Further research revealed that great leaders like Oswald Chambers, Martin Luther, and Nelson Mandela spoke of feeling distant from God and wanting to close the gap.

Not long ago Baylor University began an exhaustive study of Christian Americans and sought to measure how engaged we believe God is in the world. While the research is ongoing, some preliminary results are alarming. The data showed that 6 percent of Christians believe in a critical God who is judgmental but not engaged, and 23 percent believe in a distant God who is completely removed from our daily lives.

Luther believed most of us will pass through these dark nights, and that during these times we learn from Scripture to look beyond our experiences, feelings, and thoughts in order to contend for the faith. The solution, he said, is to allow tribulation to drive us to prayer and Scripture, but above all, to God's promises.

Although it was comforting to know I was not alone in my feelings at the time, and I better understood what I was going through, this knowledge did not release me from the darkness. I kept crying out, "God, can you hear me?"

Earlier I wrote that I know my relationship with God. I know that on days when I am lonely, I long to be in the presence of the Lord. When I am feeling odd, fat, unwanted, or displaced, I need Him to hold me. When I'm feeling the overwhelming responsibility of being a 9/11 survivor, I need a place of rest.

I need to hear Him say, "Yes, baby, I know." And because I love Him so much, there is in me an intense craving for daily contact with Him. No amount of intellectualizing or "knowing" will soothe the ache in my belly when there is a lack of feeling.

I suffered from asthma when I was young. It was pretty severe. When I had an asthma attack, my mother would put me in bed with her, medicate me, rub my chest, and pray or sing to me until I fell asleep. Somehow just being near her provided comfort and made me feel a whole lot better.

I believe it's that way with most people. It's only natural that when you love someone, you want to be with that someone. Their presence is soothing. It's not enough to know they are in the same house with you; you want to occupy the same space and "feel" them.

If you are happily married, is simply knowing that your spouse is somewhere in the house enough of a relationship for you? It might be comforting many times, but for the most part, you want interaction. You want touch.

I know I do. And so I prayed, "God, my Father, I need to feel you in and through me again. Will you come?"

Several days later I was on my knees before God, begging Him for a holy visitation. I lay on my face calling Him, the Nazarene, yearning for His touch. In my spirit I was almost daring Him to make himself known to me. He called me on that dare. And before long, I was a puddle of goop—lying there absent from myself, experiencing a precious moment and a milestone in our relationship. I "felt" Him. My toes curled, my tongue started flapping, and I heard myself pray in tongues for the first time.

This did not immediately end my period of dark nights. However, it did provide much-needed encouragement to continue living through them. For in that moment, when I felt the presence of the Holy Spirit of Jesus, my love for the Lord and His love for me were undeniable.

I'm not sure if a journey through a dark night of the soul is something every believer in Jesus Christ will need to take. Nor do I contend that all feelings of separation from God indicate such a journey. I do believe, however, that these dark nights give way to brighter days and new life.

And while these dark nights may very well be designed to help separate us from worldly desire and bring us more in line with God's purpose, I believe God's call to us is not complicated. He calls us to be holy (1 Peter 1:13–16), and the path by which He takes us to that end will vary from one person to the other.

Personally, if this dark night of the soul is the road I must travel to separate from the world and be holy, I am willing to drop all my baggage to lighten the load.

And so I go, though not as gracefully as I would always like. Just as there will be times when I hear the voice of God speak loud and clear—and I go around quoting Scripture, speaking in tongues, and feeling His love throughout my soul—there will be times when

God is quiet and I go kicking, screaming, and complaining all the daylong.

But I rest secure, looking forward to those moments when I only need to know that my Father is in the house.

Whatever the case, I resign myself to living through these times with as much grace as He will give, and alas, I find peace in that. For it is true, it is not as important to know where God is as that He knows where I am.

Amen and amen.

8

BLESSED BEYOND MEASURE

GOD IS NEAR

Have you ever reached the end of a busy day and lain down in bed to sort through your accomplishments, but instead started counting the things you didn't get done? Somehow you got so busy with—well, you can't recall exactly what occupied your time, but it was something, all right. *Where did the day go?!* One minute you're waking up and looking forward to the day, and the next minute you're lying down in the evening wondering what happened—maybe to the entire year.

With life flying by so fast, it can feel like it's all outside of God's control, or even His awareness.

Ah, there's the rub. Maybe it's not so much that we struggle with whether or not God loves us, but that we doubt He really is interactive, in control, and paying attention to us, each and every day.

Several years ago, during the Gulf War, the song "From a Distance" became popular. It combined Bette Midler's powerful voice, an arresting melody, and a seemingly spiritual context. The song stole the radio airwaves and hearts of America, shooting to #1 in its first month of release. Now, I admit I was one of those struggling souls who belted out this song when it came over the radio. Tears would fill my eyes thinking about those brave guys at war. Also at that time in my life, the chorus "God is watching us ... from a distance" was powerful and actually encouraging. It seemed to express a common belief—God is distant, but at least He's watching.

These days, I'm singing a much different tune. While I agree that in His vastness God is above all, He is much more than a passive observer. He is much more than some mysterious spiritual being who spun the world into existence and then propped His feet up on His throne to watch us for all eternity "from a distance."

I know oftentimes it can *feel* like God is far away, but the Bible is very clear that our God is an up-close, personal, all-hands-on-deck, active Savior who is very near to us. In fact, He lives with us. John 14:23 says, "All who love me will do what I say. My Father will love them, and we will come and make our home with each of them" (NLT).

I believe that! With all of my heart and soul, I believe that God lives with me, and every day He is engaged in all I do.

You can even catch me giggling sometimes when I catch Him at work. *Watch God*, I'll remind myself. And sure enough, I'll notice one thing happens to me just as something else connects to provide what is needed, and when I trace it back, I can clearly see the if-I-hadn't-done-this-I-wouldn't-have-been-there-and-that-wouldn't-have-happened-wow-God! moment.

That's what happened earlier this month. I had been sitting in my living room, fighting my way through the mental aerobics we all go through when money problems find a way into our lives. I was trying to figure how to spread a tiny bit of money over the next few weeks. It looked pretty hopeless, and I was kicking myself for not being smarter with my finances.

Then my phone rang. It was a friend whom I hadn't heard from in months. She was in my area and wanted to meet for lunch, on her tab! I happily agreed, and she suggested a very nice French café–type restaurant on the waterfront I had heard wonderful things about.

By the time we got there, the place was packed. We had just enough time to enjoy lunch and a nice conversation before the dinner crowd started to arrive. As we were leaving, though, I ran into another old pal from back in the day. He had moved to Maryland after 9/11 and was only in town for a day visiting family. Well, it turned out he had heard I was now active in ministry and asked if I would speak at his church. Ten days later we had figured out all the details and I received their generous honorarium.

Now, I'm not sure what you see at work here, but the Lord was certainly there for me . . . making sure I was where I needed to be in order to receive what He had for me and to hopefully bless others as well. If that's not active participation, I don't know what is. God provided help for me, both as a symbol through which I could learn and as an actual, personal presence in my life. And not just for me, but for those watching as well. You see, God will always take full advantage of every situation, making sure He reaches as many lives as possible.

I am assured that His presence is always right here, right now, all the time. And any sense of separation is an illusion, introduced to me by the enemy of my soul. Amen and amen.

I am sure that if you survey your life, you will find that on more than one occasion, some little thing "just happened" to connect the dots for you as well. And I hope that experience reassures you that God is not only watching you, He is living with you every day, sharing in an emotionally, spiritually, and physically intimate relationship.

For even more reassurance, one of my favorite Scripture verses is Jeremiah 29:13: "You will seek me and find me when you seek me with all your heart." I like the way that feels going down.

Another one is Psalm 139:7–18. This one is a little longer, but if you ever find yourself wandering through the house, needing confirmation that He is there, this is a good passage to reread:

Where can I go from Your Spirit? Or where can I flee from Your presence? If I ascend into heaven, You are there; if I make my bed in hell, behold, You are there. If I take the wings of the morning, and dwell in the uttermost parts of the sea, even there Your hand shall lead me, and your right hand shall hold me. If I say, "Surely the darkness shall fall on me," even the night shall be light about me; indeed, the darkness shall not hide from You, but the night shines as the day; the darkness and the light are both alike to You. For you formed my inward parts; You covered me in my mother's womb. I will praise You, for I am fearfully and wonderfully made; marvelous are Your works, and that my soul knows very well. My frame was not hidden from You, when I was made in secret, and skillfully wrought in the lowest parts of the earth. Your eyes saw my substance, being yet unformed. And in Your book they all were written, the days fashioned for me, when as yet there were none of them. How precious also are your thoughts to me, O God!

How great is the sum of them! If I should count them, they would be more in number than the sand; when I awake, I am still with You (NKJV).

God is never distant and He is never *not* with us. All we need to do is pause more and pay attention. Look for Him and enjoy His input, because in the long run, the presence and involvement of the Holy Spirit of God are all there is.

Then, finally, taking comfort in His nearness—believing Him to be close and cultivating your relationship with Him—we recognize that in this gift of His presence, we are blessed beyond measure and we accept our wonderfully abundant lives by acknowledging it, living it, and sharing it. And, so it is.

9

THE FATHER OF MERCY

HIS GOODNESS ABOUNDS
IN EVERYDAY LIFE

Our imagination is a gift from God to be enjoyed. For me, I love to explore spiritual truths through storytelling. It's how Christ, through His parables, chose to impart so many memorable teachings. In this chapter, I'd like to share a story I wrote. Through it, I hope you'll see the gentle ways of the Lord, how His mercy and goodness are all around us, especially in the simple things of life that are so easily taken for granted. May it be food for your soul.

It was Friday night, the last day of school and the first real night of my summer vacation in 1963. The air was warm, dry, and filled with the dreamy mixture of smells from newly cut grass, firecrackers, flaming barbecue grills, and bug-be-gone sprays.

The sky was wide open and accessible. I could easily lie

down on the ground, look up, and get totally lost in just how big it all was. Daddy said God made it that way because God is a musical genius. Daddy talks like that sometimes. He is a preacher on Sundays at the storefront church on the corner.

I ate dinner quickly that night so that by dusk I could sit on my front porch and watch the streetlight pop on. Flickering its warm glow and making shadows even bigger than me, it gave us something else to dance about. Kicked back on my swing, I heard crickets, hurried car horns, and the treble sounds of my momma's laughter mixing with the baritones of Daddy's flirtation.

Ray Charles played on the stereophonic player in the living room while tall glasses of lemonade rattled to the hard-hitting piano. The Browns, who lived across the street and played in our backyard, called to their mom to see if they could stay out with me just a little while longer. We were waiting for the real lights to shine. Lightning bugs!

I was eleven years old and a spitfire—"all of God's mercy," as Momma would say. The story was that she and Daddy had tried and tried to have me for five years. The doctors told them nothing was wrong, but nothing happened. Daddy finally said that God didn't have no will for them to have a baby, and they gave up just six months before Momma felt me kick.

Anyway, my house was on the corner of an old block of houses. With beaten-up wooden shutters, wraparound porches, and steps that creaked, no one home was better than another, even though ours was the only one with a swing.

The field behind our house was huge and filled with a yellow flax weed that seemed to overtake every empty lot for miles. It was perfect for hide-and-seek . . . and baseball and handball and football and catching lightning bugs. I loved it—hanging out with the guys and doing all the stuff boys do, like racing and climbing and breaking old windows and rough-housing. Momma said it was the spirit of life in me. Daddy said it was the devil. Either way, it was just me.

Me, Danny-boy, and Bubba would stand smack-dab in the middle of that open field with bits of light swimming all around us. We chased the lightning bugs as they circled, flashed, and danced to some kind of cricket instrumental.

Momma gave us Mason jars for catching them and Daddy would poke holes through the lids so the bugs could breathe. Me and the guys would run through that field just stupid with joy and excitement. Sometimes, I'd get so happy in my body that I thought I needed to take some out of me or I would just bust open.

This was one of those nights. I ran into the field ahead of Bubba and Danny, and with a half glance over my shoulder I shouted, "My jar is so big it can hold a hundred lightning bugs, and I'm gonna catch a thousand."

"Silly thing," Bubba shouted back. "If your jar can hold a hundred, then you can only catch a hundred."

"Stop running," my momma called to me from the porch.

Pretending I couldn't hear her, I announced to the boys, "I can catch as many as I want! No jar is gonna stop me, and you can't stop me either."

I ran even faster and turned in every direction, awed by the beauty of those flying lights. I dizzied from my own spinning.

"Stop running with that jar before you trip and put your eyes out," Momma called again. This time she used her I'm-not-playing-around voice.

The first lightning bug practically winked in front of my

nose. I swiped my hand in the air and caught it, then opened my palm to see my prize. It was my daddy who taught me the art of catching them. "Never run too fast and never catch them too hard," he told me. I would cup my hand as I went for them and gently close my fingers around them.

Danny-boy used to squish them when he caught 'em. Me, I would hold my hand over the jar and open my hand lightly so that they would fly right into the jar. It worked every time, and I loved seeing all the colors they made. The random flashes of light were so cool. It was like a song . . . green . . . then off . . . yellow . . . then off . . . then green again. Better than TV.

I caught lightning bug after lightning bug that night, accompanied by the sounds of Momma's laughter, Daddy's voice, and the neighborhood coming to life. It was perfect.

Then in no time at all, the bat signal: The porch lights came on and Daddy's big old voice rang out. "Mercy Ann Joy," he called. "Come now, sweet baby girl. Time for bed."

Daddy's voice was like thunder back then, and to this day, at age thirty-five, I still love the sound of a strong man's voice. His sense of humor and flirtations are quieted a bit now by the years, but he still tickles Momma and she stills dances circles around his back while rubbing the top of his head. He still sits on that porch on Friday nights making her smile and appreciating God's musical flair with old Ray Charles records playing on the stereo.

I watch my own children now as they visit Momma and Daddy. They run around the old neighborhood, laughing, playing, catching fireflies, as they call them now.

And even though that old field is now filled with condominiums, the first night of summer vacation, the glow of summer skies, the sounds of summer nights, and the smells

of summer living are still magical. They transport me back to
that night so many years ago, when I fell asleep to the sound
of crickets outside my bedroom window, a beautiful summer
breeze pushing past my Daddy-kissed cheeks and the sight of a
thousand lightning bugs dancing in a jar.

Most times, God shares His mercy with us in moments so subtle
and intertwined with our everyday that it goes unnoticed. Closely
related is His goodness, which is so consistent we often miss it. And
yet, when we do catch a glimpse, often in hindsight, how good and
vast is His mercy.

The miracle of birth, and a little girl with a great spirit. The
awareness of God's artistry, open skies, neighbors who become family, the devotion of a loving couple, children, grandchildren, music,
and, yes, even lightning bugs.

And so my prayer for us today, as we breeze through life possibly
overlooking the wonders of God, is that we always remember that
God's mercy abounds in the simplicity of our everyday lives.

Surely goodness and mercy shall follow *you* all the days of
your life; and you will dwell in the house of the Lord for ever (see
Psalm 23:6).

10

THE GOD OF ALL COMFORT

A GOD WE CAN SEE

My son, Eliot, attended Christian schools most of his life. When he was in kindergarten, each day included reading, writing, and naptime, plus fifteen minutes of Bible stories.

I remember one day when Eliot came home upset. He was concerned that two invisible people, Goo-Dess and Mercy, were going to follow him the rest of his life. Eventually I looked at his handout for the day. It turned out the class had heard a story related to Psalm 23:6: "Surely goodness and mercy shall follow me all the days of my life." I tried to explain, but there was no convincing him that goodness and mercy were not people. What finally calmed him was coming to an understanding that goodness and mercy were angels. (How do you take such a wonderful vision from a child?) It was good to have them following him, we agreed; they would protect him from bad guys. Still today, if you ask Eliot about that verse, he'll have a story for you.

Our early experiences in life have a great impact on our understanding of God. We might envision Him as a God who stays close, or we might struggle with distorted images of Him. Unfortunately, connecting with the reality of who He is can be quite a task these days, especially when science has an explanation for everything ranging from the smallest flower to atomic fusion to birth. And our studies in religious science, perhaps an oxymoron itself, are at the forefront of society's latest challenge to Christianity.

The news media, as well as New Age religions and other popular cults have laid down the gauntlet before us, and we, the Christian community, have accepted the challenge to argue our Father's existence and character from an academic rather than a biblical perspective. When speaking about creation, we present the theory of concept and design. We say the presence of intelligent design proves the existence of an intelligent designer, God. Our arguments are brilliant and our dialogue powerful in its positioning that design detection methodology is not only a prerequisite in many other fields of human endeavor—including anthropology, archaeology, and forensics—it is also applicable to creation.

Impressed?

Well, bah-humbug, because in the middle of all of the noise and debate are hearts that cry out, "With all I've been told about faith and grace and earth and science and 'seeing' God in all, it still escapes me. I am broken, lost, hungry, afraid, and still searching for my 'mustard seed' that will change it all. I need a God I can see."

If that is how you feel, there is a reason. God has put eternity in our hearts (Ecclesiastes 3:11). We long to believe in God. We long to touch Him and be touched by Him. We long to know that beyond what we see, what we hear, and what we feel—despite the chaos and questions and scientific proof or lack thereof—God is present, active, and involved in our lives.

I heard a story once about a five-year-old girl who was afraid of monsters. She was in bed for the night and was alone in her room. Upstairs in the dark, lying idle, the little girl's mind began to wander. She started imagining there were monsters in her closet. Scared and upset, she called for her mother to chase the monsters away and sit with her until she fell asleep.

Mom, who was folding laundry and making lunches for the next day, was determined to comfort her baby girl and complete her chores at the same time. She called up to her little angel, explaining that she was very busy but that she would send Jesus in her stead. Mom assured her that Jesus was a much better "monster-scarer-awayer" than mommies could ever be and that He was already there with her.

After a few minutes of quiet, the little girl called back. "Mom," she said, "can you send up someone with skin on him?"

When I first heard this story, I could completely relate to the feelings of that child. I understood the need to touch the proof of my salvation. Back then my mind understood the concept of God's omnipresence, but my heart's need was to feel secure in His participation in my life. I wanted to be confident that He wasn't just watching me from afar. Like that little girl, I needed somehow to connect with Him in a way more tangible than "just believing."

Nowadays, and after more reflection, I am beginning to understand the struggle: We still believe in monsters. Furthermore, we believe our monsters are more present with us than our God is. And I think our dependency on brainpower and proof that we can see have made our faith weaker. English scholar John Selden said, "In my intellect, I may divide [faith and works], just as in the candle I know there is both light and heat; but put out the candle, and both are gone."

In Leslie's world, I understand there is both science and there is God; but take away God and . . .

Perhaps our much-evolved efforts to prove God's existence have caused us to neglect the evidence of His presence. Perhaps we have forgotten to rest—assured that God is, and that His presence, both ubiquitous and involved, has always been. Maybe, just maybe, our theological studies, though relevant, have become far too traditional and our traditions have made the Word of God have little effect. For many today, faith has become theoretical, but it is not possible to love conjecture. In Matthew 15:8–9, Jesus said, "These people draw near to Me with their mouth, and honor Me with their lips, but their heart is far from Me" (NKJV).

God gave us the Bible to be the one true pathway to a God we *can* see. The Bible does not theorize who He is. It does not argue for or try to prove God. It simply assumes Him and then goes on to reveal the God who is assumed. Without rhetoric or explanation, it begins very cleanly, "In the beginning, God . . ." Our lives pick up the assumption from there. Our existence is all the proof we should need.

And still, despite knowing this, there *are* times when we can't see God, when there seems to be a deafening silence from heaven, and no matter what we do, nothing breaks the silence.

I have lived those seemingly silent moments, where it would have been a lot easier if He would have just dressed in flesh and talked to me. And time after time I have been warned not to base my faith on my feelings or emotions. The problem is, in those times "emotional" is all that I am. I have nothing else. Sometimes when I am an emotional wreck I need an emotional response from God.

The good news: Our God, who is gracious and supportive, understands our desire for reassurance and our need for emotional response. And so I believe that for our growth and His glory, His touch will on occasion produce goose bumps, warm fuzziness, or some other emotion. I believe that knowing us as He does, He might even stir us intensely—even to graying our hair.

Consider Moses. His encounters with God were obvious and dramatic. Blessed with signs of fire, smoke, an earthquake, a burning bush, and even a voice that called him by his own name—twice (Exodus 3:4)—I'm sure Moses had no problem seeing God and trusting God's interest in him. On one occasion, Moses was even confident enough to ask God to reveal the full manifestation of His glory. In Exodus 33:21–22, God spoke to Moses, "There is a place near me where you may stand on a rock. When my glory passes by, I will put you in a cleft in the rock and cover you with my hand until I have passed by."

God responded to Moses' desire to see Him, and I believe He responds to our desire as well. In Hebrews 13:8, the Bible assures us that God is the same yesterday and today and forever. He does not change. So even in this present time of doubt and scientific scrutiny, the absolute and essential fact is that we can be confident that the glory, the majesty, and yes, the presence of the God of Moses are near us today.

I can recall a time when I desperately needed a touch from the Lord. I begged God to let me feel His heart. The response I got was much different from anything I expected. Every time I prayed, my eyes drained. I could not stop crying. An intercessor at my church explained that my heart was experiencing a small amount of the Holy Spirit's grieving.

C. H. Spurgeon had the right attitude in looking at and approaching the vastness of God: "There is something exceedingly improving to the mind in a contemplation of the Divinity. It is a subject so vast, that all our thoughts are lost in its immensity; so deep, that our pride is drowned in its infinity. . . . But while the subject humbles the mind, it also expands it. . . . I know nothing which can so comfort the soul; so calm the swelling billows of sorrow and grief; so speak peace to the winds of trial, as a devout musing upon the subject of the Godhead."

I won't deny it "feels" a lot nicer to get all warm and fuzzy "feeling" God. But once again, we are not limited to just this. In fact, the minute we conclude that our inner feelings and spiritual reality will always coincide, we are headed for disappointment. Our feelings and the reality of God's presence are not inter-reliant. We won't always dance when He brings joy. Nor will His presence always stimulate us.

I saw this in a woman I know from church. Cancer had filled her body, and the doctors said she had only six months to live. She would sit through services, clearly in pain.

That was ten years ago. Today, she is alive and well, without a smidge of cancer. She never cried or felt any warm sensations; in fact, she can't even say exactly when her healing occurred. Nevertheless, the Lord clearly moved through her body and healed her, and she has no doubt of His participatory presence in her life.

In other words, God's grace in our lives is evidence of God's presence in our lives. We don't have to wait until something is spooky or spectacular before we see Him. We shouldn't have to look for an out-of-this-world experience to know Him. We can see God in His goodness to us every day: as we lift a fork to our mouth, raise a window blind to the sun, work a job, watch a sunset, sleep through the night, or raise children. We see Him in His mercy when He enables us to survive cancer, grow beyond abuse, pray for one another, and even enjoy the cerebral capacity to challenge Him who is the giver of all this good.

Seeing and touching the God who made us is a magnificent experience that He himself has purposed for each one of us. He opens our eyes, broadens our perspective, and then reveals himself to us. And in the context of our life choices, every experience, whether ceremonial or mundane, planned or unplanned, if we remind ourselves to be aware that God is with us, He will move us beyond the need for physical manifestations and into the knowledge of truth. Emotions aside, His grace is ever present.

By His Word, His promises, His biblical examples, and yes, even His tender touch, we see Him.

And then we have our Moses moments, when we are huddled in the cleft, uncertain but hoping. We perceive what feels like a comforting hand on our shoulder, or a whisper in our ear, and we know beyond knowing that our Father is with us. We know that this is where we belong. And as He passes, His holiness causes our toes to curl, tears to fall, hands to tremble, and lips to quiver. We are speechless, except for an occasional "Yes, Lord," and we get just a glimpse of God's grace, His forgiveness, love, joy, hope, and the reassurance that can be none other than His presence. And there in the holy presence of the Lord, everything is clear as we are filled with, are one with, the Spirit of our Lord Jesus Christ. His sight and hearing becomes ours as our spirits awaken—filled with His life, His light, and His love. *Yes, Lord!*

Now, as I settle back in my easy chair, I'm remembering His goodness. And as I'm finding Him, I'm losing more of myself, understanding more of His nature. He is the Father of compassion and the God of all comfort, who comforts us in all our troubles and makes provision for our natural and spiritual needs that we might know Him.

Now His Holy Spirit reminds me that even when difficulty and struggle come our way, our experiences are not prescriptive but rather descriptive of our individual journeys toward the everlasting. Some are beautiful, some are symbolic, some are ordinary, and some are very hard to understand. Some occur because of a biblical revelation and others by way of a single falling tear. But they are all ultimately good because they point us to truth. We really do have a loving Father, a God we can see.

Indeed, from the life cycle of a perennial flower to the full life cycle of me, a little black girl from the south side of Chicago who once was afraid of monsters, both are evidences of Him. And none of God's creation is outside of His good care and perfect vision. For in the busy-ness, in the noise, in the static of our days, once we learn to slow ourselves down and quiet our minds, He becomes more visible.

———

Here's another story about seeing God. Unfortunately, the author is unknown, but it is fitting that it also speaks of the faith and honesty of a child:

A small boy once approached his slightly older sister with a question about God. "Susan, can anybody ever really see God?" Busy with other things, Susan curtly replied, "No, of course not, silly. God is so far up in heaven that nobody can see Him."

Time passed, but his question still lingered, so he approached his mother: "Mom, can anybody ever really see God?"

"No, not really," she gently said. "God is a spirit and He dwells in our hearts, but we can never really see Him." Somewhat satisfied but still wondering, the youngster went on his way.

Not long afterward, his saintly old grandfather took the little boy on a fishing trip. They were having a great time together—it had been an ideal day. The sun was beginning to set with unusual splendor as the day ended. The old man stopped fishing and turned his full attention to the exquisite beauty unfolding before him. On seeing the face of his grandfather reflecting such deep peace and contentment as he gazed into the magnificent ever-changing sunset, the little boy thought for a moment and finally spoke hesitatingly, "Grandad, I . . . I . . . wasn't going to ask anybody else, but I wonder if you can tell me the answer to something I've been wondering about a long time. Can anybody—can *anybody*—ever really see God?"

The old man did not even turn his head. A long moment slipped by before he finally answered. "Grandson," he quietly said, "it's getting so I can't see anything else."

Seeing God and receiving His comfort do not rely on science to prove or disprove who He is. It relies on our faith. We need only to slow down enough to see Him in the not-so-obvious places. Our love for Him and His love for us will reveal His face. It's no more complicated than that.

Be encouraged in your search for His face. It is certainly a beautiful one! His promise to you is that if you seek Him with all of your heart, you will find Him. And my prayer for you today is that you will see a glimpse of God that ignites the fire in your heart.

"Praise be to the God and Father of our Lord Jesus Christ, the Father of compassion and the God of all comfort, who comforts us in all our troubles, so that we can comfort those in any trouble with the comfort we ourselves have received from God" (2 Corinthians 1:3–4).

11

Embracing the Unknown

Change Equals Opportunity

Not many people like change. I remember when I first noticed that the skin on my neck wasn't as tight as it once was and that I wasn't as slim as I used to be, not as curvy, not as light on my feet. Then that first gray hair appeared. I couldn't get it pulled out quick enough! It wasn't long after that when I realized that those fifteen-minute power naps that used to get me up and at 'em now caused me to miss the entire afternoon.

I heard someone say once that life happens while we're off doing something else. Normal things in the course of human events can turn our entire world upside down. We age, the children are suddenly college students who move away to begin their own lives, old friends and relatives die, we get sick or laid off from work, and that big old drafty house we grew up in has to be sold in favor of a more manageable, less-expensive one.

As much as I would like to keep some things as they once were, I understand that life demands change. I don't know about you, but I'd prefer that my life changes were introduced slowly—and with an instruction manual.

That's probably the general consensus. By nature we want things to be steady and predictable. We want our lives to be uninterrupted and not given to the shake-ups that a godly life demands. But not only is this not biblical, it is not practical.

You see, God purposes change in our lives so that we might learn from Him and be more like Him. And because most of us are experiential learners, He also purposes that the changes are introduced by external forces. He knows that in order for us to really get it, we need to get our hands involved in each lesson He has for us. We need to touch it, feel it, and live it in order to own the lesson.

It's simple, really. Think about one of life's earliest lessons, usually taught by mothers everywhere: "The Stove Can Burn You." Auditory learners heard their mother, believed the information, and never touched the stove. Visual learners watched their brother touch the stove, and never touched it themselves. But experiential learners, which comprise more than 60 percent of us, touched the stove—but only once!

In order to be doers of the Word and not hearers only, we have to be moved from our old ways by "touching the stove"—living the change.

My sister Lanita was an alcoholic and a drug addict for many years. I never knew her to try rehab or any program to help her with her problem. In fact, most of her conversations about her addictions were outright denial. For years she was seemingly determined to kill herself and would do almost anything to get her high. She hung around the same people, played the same games, used the same drugs, and got nowhere in her life.

It was sometimes difficult to look at my sister, once beautiful and full of hope and laughter, begin to lose her teeth. Her skin showed more than her years, and her body was slowing down from all the wear and tear. I can't speak for my other siblings, but honestly, as painful as it is to admit, I thought my sister would die on drugs.

Late in the fall of 2002, Lanita was about to be evicted from her apartment. Although my family, especially my nephew Larry, wanted to help, she was too far behind in the rent and there was nothing anyone could do to make a difference. Then one day she surprised us all by leaving Chicago altogether.

Not even six months later, Lanita had her own apartment and a new job, and was clean and sober. She had given her life to the Lord, and He had performed a complete 180-degree change in her life. She had become a living example that sometimes what looks like a bad change on the surface can bring about miraculous changes on the inside!

God changed my sister's living situation in order to change her environment, in order to change her!

God purposely introduces change outwardly in all of our lives in order to also change us on the inside. He wants to change our ways of thinking, to get us to let go of our traditions in favor of the Word of God, to open our eyes to the wonders of His truth, to help us to embrace the reality and power of faith so that we can live abundant lives. Colossians 3:9–10 says, "You have put off the old man with his deeds, and have put on the new man who is renewed in knowledge according to the image of Him who created him" (NKJV).

Our life changes are to be the pathway to unparalleled opportunities for growth and catalysts for transformation that redefine our soul's mission and stretch us beyond our flesh. It's like getting a do-over.

That's exactly what He did in Lanita's life. And now, more than six years later, and after more than twenty years of addiction, praise God, my beautiful sister is still clean and sober, still in church, still working, and as of last year was dating a deacon. Now, that's really cool! And that's change!

Paul explains in the twelfth chapter of Romans that we should not be conformed to this world but rather be transformed by the renewing of our mind, so that we may prove what the will of God is, that which is good and acceptable and perfect (v. 2). That's change!

Mark Twain said, "Twenty years from now, you will be more disappointed by the things that you didn't do than by the ones you did do. So throw off the bowlines. Sail away from the safe harbor. . . . Explore. Dream. Discover."

Isn't that so much of the beauty in life—the dreaming, exploring, discovering. But we must allow change in order to live the dream. We must grow in order to discover it, and we must embrace change in order to live life!

And as we embrace the change, the Holy Spirit reminds us that change is opportunity and opportunity is good. And though things change, God does not change (James 1:17).

When God blesses you with opportunity in the form of change, don't fight against, take it. Don't try to understand it; His ways are not our ways. Don't make it a spiritual battle. Just embrace it! More often than not, He's moving you into a new direction.

My sister Laverne is very sweet and honest and has a natural mothering instinct. Laverne owns a small printing business, which to me isn't quite what she is supposed to do. Recently her business slowed a bit and she immediately started looking for other work. She reassessed her skills and desires, sent out résumés, solicited prayer from family and friends, and tried to be exactly where she thought God wanted her in order to take advantage of any opportunity. I didn't have the heart to tell her that she was already doing it. For months, Laverne had been actively working with my brother to build up his new church. She was already balancing the church's financial books, traveling with me on speaking trips, and supporting her son and his new fiancée after she unexpectedly lost her mother.

God was already making full use of Laverne's unique strengths, gifts, and natural talents, which could only surface and be appreciated because of the changes. She didn't lose her business, she gained in the area of ministry. She didn't lose herself, she gained her true self.

You see, change and loss are two different things. While loss will take from our lives, change will often bring increase, particularly when God is in it! God was already providing for my sister as well as providing for the lives of those she touched. Although we can't stop change or loss from occurring, we can determine our place within them. If we wait on Him, God will not let us miss the opportunity or the gift or the miracle that He has purposed for us.

Being a single woman, I have many single friends. And most of us have dated a frog or two all the while knowing he was a frog. We simply ignored his "frogdom," decided we could fix him, and convinced ourselves it would be our kiss that turned him into the wonderful prince. Well, not so much.

You see, that's not biblical. Why are we always so willing to settle for so much less than what God has planned for us? The Bible tells us, "Blessed is the man who listens to me, watching daily at my doors, waiting at my doorway" (Proverbs 8:34).

Position yourself in spirit so that you can hear God's communication to you. Sanctify yourself, get into His courts, turn from the din and clamor of the world, submerge yourself in His holy presence, and then . . . wait. Know that God does not author confusion. If you are confused about an action or decision, then God is not in it. I promise you, He is not some great divine riddler that we have to figure out in order to find the opportunities He is sending our way. His yoke is easy. His ways are plain, they are straight—and we'll recognize them, because "His works are perfect" (Deuteronomy 32:4). Yes, and God's ways are just! God's plans are perfect! Say this to yourself: "God's ways are just, and God's works are perfect!" And then remember it. Write yourself a note and post it on your refrigerator if you have to, but remember that the situations we face in life—even when life-threatening or soul-drenching—are but thresholds to something else.

I honestly believe we don't have to worry! As we embrace change, we will find the opportunities within it. We adjust our focus from the thing that is changing to the thing that is approaching, and then miraculously, what was once the cause of your losing your breath amazingly becomes a breath of hope.

We walk confidently away from one phase of life toward another, looking forward to the days that lie ahead. We no longer worry about what should have, could have, or would have been, and we rejoice in this season of change. Our fear of life dissipates and no longer binds us to the past. We become reassured that whatever waits just beyond those doors will continue to mold us into vessels of liberation—not only for ourselves but for others as well.

My uncle passed from this life not long ago. His death shook my cousin so much that he sought out a program that focused on spiritual healing, which led to his leaving Islam for Christianity. Given new horizons, we discover new things. We become new people!

Just last night, during a phone conversation with my cousin, he ended a long pause by singing, "Jesus, He Will Fix It." His new life inspired a poem I'd like to share with you. As you read, my prayer is that you will begin dreaming, exploring, discovering, and changing.

Mercy Through the Looking Glass

Sweet smiles and careful grins
Shine through the glass and through the gates
Yesterday the chains were there
Today liberation
Waits
Quietly
Suddenly
Quickly
Through dream-soaked promises
The existence of mercy is finally realized
And discovered
And lived
Through the looking glass
Yea,
Through the looking glass

12

HAVE FAITH IN GOD

THERE IS NO SPOON

Blaise Pascal wrote, "Faith certainly tells us what the senses do
not, but not the contrary of what they see; it is above, not against
them."

One of my favorite sermons to hear is any message on faith. I
never tire of being encouraged to live a life pleasing before God.
So last week, when I visited one of the charismatic churches in
my area, I was thrilled to sit in an old wooden pew and peep over
a lady's tall hat to hear the preacher begin his sermon from the
eleventh chapter of Mark. Embellishing his opening words, the
Scripture text was Mark 11:22–24, where Jesus is teaching about
living by faith. Jesus says, "Have faith in God. . . . If anyone says
to this mountain, 'Go, throw yourself into the sea,' and does not
doubt in his heart but believes that what he says will happen, it
will be done for him."

The preacher told us the troubles we experience in life are like mountains. But if we have enough faith, we can speak to the mountain and demand it to move out of our way, and the mountain will obey. The response from the congregation was more than indicative of how people in general are searching for any glimmer of hope. I wish I could fully describe it. People were on their feet clapping, dancing, and singing. I, too, felt uplifted by the message.

But in hindsight, I wonder how many of us in that church or elsewhere fully understand faith. We read in the Bible that faith moves mountains, the just live by it, and it is the substance of things hoped for and the evidence of things unseen. But what does it all mean?

Faith is often thought of in terms of trusting God through tough times no matter the circumstances. But the simplicity of trust is only the beginning.

I would argue that we should go deeper now and gain a richer understanding of the faith that moves mountains. And though I am keenly aware that living this "out loud" is no easy task, I am persuaded that it is possible. You see, God has already given to each man a good measure of faith (Romans 12:3), so trusting God is the easy part; living faith is the hard part.

I'll explain. Contrary to what many believe, faith and trust are not the same. Faith is the extension of trust. While trust answers our questions, faith poses more. Trust is a confidence in what can be proven; faith is an assurance of what cannot.

Trust is not manifested in action. Even if we accept the possibility that our mental acts, decisions, and choices are lined up somehow to trust, trust in itself is something completely different. It is something that is not primarily a question of action. It is an act of our own will. We decide to trust.

Faith is not like that. It is not related to a decision or to choice, but rather to a state of absence of choice. You do not decide to have faith. We don't make the choice to have faith after mulling over the consequences of not having it.

And as you give yourself over to trust, faith compels you to let go! Faith is quite simply letting go—with no objective reason— it simply is what it is, and you have to live it. You see, the moment it admits an objective, it ceases to be faith. Thus faith is the unquestioned surrender to the will of the Almighty God and a quiet strength to face life just as it is—whatever it is.

For example, recently I was on my way to Charlotte to speak. For some reason, I was a little more anxious than usual to fly. Leading up to my trip, I had talked to God a lot, but I was still a bit of a mess.

The morning of my flight, I went into Eliot's room and woke him to give him my itinerary and to say good-bye. Knowing that I had been having a few issues all week, he opened his eyes and looked at me through mounds of sleep and said, "See ya later, Mom. Don't worry, you'll be all right. But if not, I'll be all right." And so, my friends, there you have it—straight from the mouths of babes.

While trust will indeed compel us to keep moving forward, faith disconnects us from our desired outcomes so that we can embrace whatever God has planned. In living by faith, we become fully vested in the present because we know the future is going to be fine, no matter what.

We know that as long as we live, life will keep happening. We know that in this life there will be disappointment, but if we put our trust in God's promise and our faith in God—laying aside every weight and receiving into our souls every breathable moment with the unshakable conviction that God is totally and spotlessly upright—He will carry us through. That's faith! A lifestyle that speaks directly to our Creator God and nothing of this world.

So no matter what our circumstances are or how things appear, the truth is that God is, God does, God says, and therefore it is. . . .

One of my favorite movies is *The Matrix*. The hero, Neo, is on a journey to understand life. As he begins to realize there is a vast reality beyond the one he can see and understand, his abilities increase. As he gains a deeper understanding of what is real, he defeats his enemy.

In one scene, Neo meets a young boy. The boy has a spoon and is bending it without physical force. Intrigued, Neo asks how it's done. The boy replies, "Do not try to bend the spoon. That's impossible. Instead, only try to realize the truth: There is no spoon."

Faith is like that. Perhaps we can say that the troubles we face in life really are represented as mountains. And perhaps we really can speak to them. But, knowing that faith moves mountains *only* when we understand that in the vastness of life, beyond what we can see . . . limitless . . . bigger than what our minds can even grasp, there really is no mountain.

13

HE CARES

BIG GOD . . . LITTLE THINGS

Sunday was a tough one for me. What started out as a quiet morning quickly evolved into a situation that involved police officers, a neighbor who needed help, her abusive husband, and me. By the time I lay down at the end of the day, I was spent and wondering where God was in all of that.

As I lay there in bed, I thought about the deliverance stories in the Old Testament—miracles that up our expectations of God to huge rescues, burning bushes, parting seas, escapes from lions' dens, massive floods, big boats, giants and slingshots, and even freedom marches.

We learn from these to expect big things from Him. When in distress, we call to Him and expect our deliverances to be just as dramatic as those of old. We pray, half expecting the doors to our homes to blow wide open with angels riding in on whistling winds, while the God of our mind arrives on a cloud with fire and brimstone. And the whole world will know that the God of Abraham does amazing things in our lives.

Well, not so much. Although I am impressed by a God of wonders, I am even more moved by a God who is engaged in our everyday lives—in the little things. This is where we need Him most.

We need Him to walk with us through this world where life can go from 0 to 150 in seconds, and while it's comforting to think about the hugeness of God, I believe it is more endearing to think about the God of the universe knowing each of us, caring about us as individuals, and walking with us through our daily joys and challenges. I need to know Him like that.

And so a few days ago, He responded to the questions of my heart.

As I took my hike through the mountains, I noticed the immensity of God much more than usual. From the rocks and snow on the ground to the vastness I saw while gazing across a clear, bright, blue sky, it was beyond words. I was in awe of Him, realizing that the same God who designed all of that designed me too.

His big hands and gentle heart created the universe and the flower, molded the mountains and a baby's smile. God's eyes saw me and you and all the planets at once. And the same God who put the sky in its place and spins things in orbit also rescues the brokenhearted.

I love God when He does that; I mean, surrounding me with the truth that is. Just when I'm right in the middle of myself, He saves me yet again. And what I learn every time is that these are the times that if I'll listen, God has much to say.

Throughout the Bible, the stories suggest that while God is indeed Jehovah God—God of the big stories, the healings, and great transformations—He is also the God of all comfort, who desires intimacy with us and to get involved in the smallest details of our lives. This is evident in the selection of Rebekah as Isaac's wife (Genesis 24), the pillar of cloud by which He guided the Israelites daily in the wilderness (Numbers 9), instructions for David when his wife and children were taken captive (1 Samuel 30), His advice to Jesus regarding the selection of the apostles (Luke 6), and His decisions about where Paul should preach (Acts 16:9–10).

And He is the same God today.

A few weeks ago, my dear friend Veva shared a powerful story with me. It was early fall and her daughter Lauren had been looking around the house all season for her favorite jacket but couldn't find it. Weeks passed and Lauren had long since given up her search. Then while doing some work in a different part of the house, Veva came upon the jacket, and while Lauren was out, she put it on Lauren's bed for her to find. When Lauren came home from school, she found the jacket on her bed and was thrilled. And it was perfect timing, too, because later that evening the temperature in Chicago really dropped.

There is a lot to be learned from stories like these if we stop and take notice of what is really going on around us.

God cares about even the tiny things of our lives. He loves us so much that He has taken the time to know us intimately. In Isaiah 49:16, God tells us, "I have engraved you on the palms of my hands," while Psalms 56:8 (NKJV) reminds us that He collects our tears in a bottle. Surely this is a God who is not too big for the details!

And so by week's end, I sat near my fireplace warming my tired bones and surveying the landscape for the subtle blessings that I might have missed or rushed past in anticipation of the next best, latest, and greatest. As I glanced back over the journey of this past year, most of it now a blur, I know it has been lived with Christ at the helm and filled with the wonders of His obvious grace.

I am grateful that the year has reunited me with old friends, brought me new ones, and hinted at long-awaited dreams being fulfilled. I've launched a new Web site, expanded my Safe HUGS ministry, and even discovered new ways to be a more gentle light.

Overall, I've learned some pretty cool things about how to grow my spiritual self, and I have become more attentive to the voice of God.

And I find that in the middle of the bazillion tiny moments of my unpredictable and busy life of *doing*, God has undergirded me with the quiet persistence of His good works and evidence of everyday miracles: sunrises, sunsets, friends to laugh with, birthday flowers to appreciate, hot tea at bedtime, dogs to pet, and warm socks to put on. Again, in His gentle way, He reveals a life blessed beyond measure and screaming with evidence of His concern over the little things.

And yes, sometimes His concern will appear via the thunder, rushing winds, fire and brimstone. But most times it will come quietly in a song that touches your heart, or while walking in the rain, or lying on your back and gazing up into the heavens, or in the warm kiss of a puppy.

Where was God for me last Sunday? Right where He should have been—in the middle of it all. You see, that Sunday evening, in the glow of warm lights and a crackling fire, He came via the calming voice of a new friend who brought me gentle wisdom spoken with love. And I thank Him.

So listen for God, my friends. Survey the landscape, slow down, and watch with great expectation for the rescue that will surely come . . . and remember the little things!

Let me pray for us.

Heavenly Father,

I thank you that you are big enough to hold the universe together with your thoughts and small enough to hold us together with your love. God of Abraham, Isaac, and Jacob, we confess that you are the God of our lives as well, bringing miracles by fire and miracles by a gentle kiss. Open our eyes that we might see your glory in all things and give thanks.

In the name of Him whom we seek,

Amen.

14

GOD'S LITTLE MIRACLES

DARCY'S STORY

Lately, I've been challenging myself to embrace changes in my life by paying attention to God and all of His wonders. Specifically I'm looking for all the niceties that He gives—the everyday little kisses that I'd otherwise miss because I'm waiting for His hug. I'm usually distracted by the next latest and greatest derailment to come my way. And for some reason, perhaps that human thing again, I can't walk away from my crisis moments without an explanation. Consequently, nothing short of a miracle will move me in times like these.

When we think of miracles, what usually come to mind are the Red-Sea, Burning-Bush, Life-From-the-Dead types. But there are other miracles—the up-close-and-personal ones that demonstrate God's love in small things, like finding something or someone we lost, remembering a family member's birthday, witnessing a bird experience the wide-open sky, meeting that special someone, seeing a flower newly opened, and receiving a nice Hallmark card for no reason at all.

These are the ones that move me. And Darcy's story was borne from those.

I wrote Darcy's story as a parable. I don't know where you are in your life right now, or what you need from God, but I hope that in this story you see as Darcy does—that the big picture of God's perfect plan is drawn by the hands of tiny miracles.

The colors that draped the horizon caught her eye. As she stared out the window, she heard herself inhale. The trees rushed by in the distance, and as her scenic journey unfolded she couldn't help but take it all in.

The time was somewhere between dusk and dreams as the train began its gradual climb into the mountains. And with a picturesque view of the rushing river below it, it was spectacular. Thin, white aspen trees with shimmering leaves lined the grassy hills and wildlife grazed in the pasture. As the train climbed higher, the backward view revealed the entire valley. She exhaled. Darcy had waited all her life for this trip.

"Are you okay?" she heard a voice ask.

Turning to her left, she noticed for the first time that a plump, mature-looking woman had sat beside her. A quick scan of her fashion sense and hairstyle revealed that she was a very earthy soul, sixtyish, with more of an eye for color in character than in wardrobe. Darcy was on the conservative side.

Darcy stared out the window again and watched the trees slide by on both sides. As the train picked up speed it began its gentle swaying, which she thought must have felt like being rocked to sleep in a cradle—that slow-motion movement, the head wobbling back and forth in perfect rhythm with the bouncing and leaning of the train. She relaxed into it and waited for her good-night.

The woman poked her in the side. "Did you hear me, girl?"

Darcy turned. "Huh? What did you say?"

"Where you going?" The plump lady turned to face Darcy. She pulled from a Baggie a sandwich that was cut in two and took a bite.

Darcy couldn't help but notice the smell of cheese and dry meat. She turned her nose and lifted her brow. "Excuse me?" she replied.

"Where—you—going?"

I'm going where the train is going, is what Darcy wanted to say, but instead she grumbled, "I'm on my way to Idaho Falls."

"Oh. You going home or leaving home?"

"Both," Darcy replied.

"Oh, you're one of those wisenheimers, huh? I'll leave you alone then. Just tryin' to make conversation."

The motion of the train changed as it moved around a sharp corner, hugging a sheer rock face. Several trees swerved close to the tracks and then away again in graceful arcs. Alpine meadows sprinkled with wildflowers seemed to jump into view from nowhere and tall, dark green conifers framed the spectacular vistas. Darcy surveyed the horizon and then her life. Her mind went immediately to the reason she was going to Idaho Falls, and she remembered her mother. Darcy was only eight when the Department of Children and Family Services took her away. Her mom was thought to be bipolar, and social workers claimed she was unable to care for Darcy.

Since then, life had always been huge for Darcy, something to fear. Court records showed that her mom never fought the complaint or the removal. And all of her life, Darcy wondered why. Now after thirty years of questions, she was about to get her answers.

That special sound trains make rang in her ears and through the soles of her feet. It was soothing to Darcy, but before she could completely relax into the lull of it all, her thoughts were interrupted.

"You spending Christmas there? Hope yours is going to be better than the looks of mine."

Darcy looked at the woman straight on. "Look," she said, "I'm not trying to be rude or anything, but I'm really not the warm, fuzzy talkative type. I'd just like to ride this train until I get to where I'm going without the pressure of polite conversation, staying awake, or adding another friend to the already too long roster of friends that I never call now."

The lady took a huge cookie from her bag and bit into it. "No chance of any of those things happening," the lady responded.

Darcy talked over her. "Are we clear?" she asked, looking around the train car, just in case she had witnesses.

"Oh, I don't know. I'm still a little foggy on what happens in a person's life to make them so bottled up inside."

Darcy's eyes widened. Glancing nervously around, she turned to face the lady, and with one hand over her heart and the other one over her mouth, she asked, "What is wrong with you? Why don't you just leave me alone?"

The lady just looked at Darcy and smiled. "Okay," she said. "Don't get yourself worked up into a huff. My name is Nana, and I'll be sitting right here if you change your mind—about adding to that list of yours, I mean."

"Right," Darcy said while turning to look out the window

again. By then she was so worked up that she almost felt like she had to catch up on what she had missed. She forced herself to relax again into the peaceful quiet of the scenery. Watching everything slip by was incredibly pacifying. Leaning her head back and closing her eyes, she recalled her mom's beautiful face as clear now in her mind as it was back then in her reality. Darcy even remembered the yellow dress her mom wore the last time she saw her.

It was on a dreary December morning, just two days before Christmas, when the caseworkers knocked on the door of their small duplex. Darcy told the strangers her mother wasn't home and then shut the door. Twenty minutes later, they returned. Three caseworkers and two police officers entered the home, ordered Darcy to pack a few things, and drove her away.

Darcy remembered how lonely she felt, looking through the car's back window. "Mommy," she cried as the car pulled away.

Now she struggled not to cry at the memory. Disturbed by her own fidgeting, she opened her eyes and repositioned herself in her seat.

Darcy's movement got Nana's attention, but Nana said nothing. She knew from years of living that sooner or later, Darcy would want to talk. She'd seen this kind before—strong, determined, focused, and still afraid. She'd seen the walls of defense. She knew that they would eventually fall, that they needed to fall. "Be quick or be dead," Nana blurted out, " 'cause fear will never let you live."

Darcy didn't budge. She didn't even open her eyes. But after trying to fight back tears, she soon felt warm liquid trails sliding down her cheeks. She was annoyed with herself for being so vulnerable. She could think of no reason for feeling the way she did or for crying. None at all. In many ways, her life had been good.

After being taken away from her mother, she had spent only one night in a facility and two weeks in foster care. Darcy was then adopted by an upper-middle-class family. She attended private schools and had the best of everything. She graduated college with honors, married a doctor nine years her senior, and had spent the past eighteen years being loved dearly by her husband. Aside from all her charity work, Darcy volunteered tirelessly, helping a woman with bipolar disorder. Her husband supported her in all her efforts.

But something was missing for Darcy. The early separation from her mother had left her feeling empty. Emotionally there had been no healing all those years, and she could not open her heart completely to anyone. Darcy was filled with pain. The tears streamed.

Nana reached over to Darcy and put her hand on her knee. "There, there," she said.

Darcy quickly grabbed Nana's wrist and pushed her hand away. "Listen, lady, how many times do I have to tell you. I don't want to talk to you. If you don't leave me alone, I'm going to ask the conductor to move my seat."

"And where would you go, where you wouldn't be . . ." Nana asked calmly.

"Just leave me alone," Darcy said, her voice cracking. She crossed her arms and scooted closer to the window, all but shutting herself off from Nana.

"Suit yourself, but whatever has you crying now will have you crying again later, unless you let some light in. God—"

Darcy interrupted before Nana could finish. "God what?" she said in annoyance.

The very mention of God's name pierced Darcy's heart like a sword. She opened her eyes and turned to look at Nana. Again, straight on. "I know you are not about to try talking to me about God, especially after I told you not to talk to me at all, lady. Seriously, are you crazy?"

Nana responded, "Some think so."

"Besides," Darcy said, "I don't need your God. I am happy and perfectly content. And the last thing I need is to go on some endless search for an elusive divine purpose that only a hidden God knows, and will or won't reveal to me, depending on how much I suffer and beg for it. I don't need any handout, thank you. Nothing will change my life."

"But why would you want to change your life?" Nana asked calmly. "I'd think you'd be more interested in changing what you're vested in . . . like *you*. And you're right; you can find happiness in life without having God. But no matter how happy you are right now, or later on, your life would be a lot more fulfilling with God in it.

"Knowing God doesn't change your life," Nana continued. "It changes *you*. And that's the huge difference. Think of it this way. Riding a bike is a lot of fun to a child, but when he grows up he'll want to learn how to drive a car. After that, biking might seem boring. See, you only *think* you've got it all right now because you're looking at life from behind the handlebars of a bike."

Darcy paused in contemplation. Her spirit calmed a little, and she felt herself warm to Nana. Deep within, her soul was beginning to open to the mysteries of God, and her heart was being touched by the gentle and Holy Spirit of God saying, "I love you and I'm here for you."

Taking notice of Darcy's openness, Nana invited more interest by taking out a small worn paperback and softly humming "Amazing Grace." As Darcy listened, she was moved. She sniffed and searched in her small Gucci handbag for a tissue. Blowing her nose softly and very ladylike, as she'd been taught, Darcy turned again to look at Nana. Never before had she found herself in such a vulnerable place, and with a complete stranger. She was uncomfortable, but for once, willing.

"Whatever it is, it's gonna be all right, child," encouraged Nana. Darcy made a sound like an exhaled sigh of relief and a question mark at the same time.

"I'm not surprised that God put us together," Nana said.

"Why?"

" 'Cause you want to meet Him."

"Meet who?" Darcy asked.

"You want to meet Jesus."

Nana's statement was met with sharpness. "No I don't." Backing down a bit, Darcy added, "I just want to know why He hates me so much."

Then, just like in the movies, twilight's last gleam of light shone through the window on Nana's face—round, gentle, and wise. And the evening, stirred only by the breath of one soul searching, fell silent. Moonlight began to wash over everything in the train car and reflected Darcy's final call for help.

Nana spoke in her softest tone. "God doesn't hate you, dear. He loves you. He loves you and He wants to be a part of your everyday life. Do you really think it would make sense for Him to put so much into creating you and providing for your life's fulfillment if He hated you?" Nana paused and reached over again to touch Darcy on the knee as she had before. This time Darcy allowed it.

"Even if you don't understand all that God has allowed in your life, surely you understand that it was not He who actually did it. He's a fixer, not a breaker," Nana said.

"Then why did He allow so much ugliness in my life? He took my mother away. He trapped me in depression all of my life, and now you're asking me to believe that He has my best interests at heart? If that were true, why would He have it in such confusion?"

"Oh, so you do have a knowledge of God?" asked Nana.

"Everybody knows about God."

"Ah, but not everybody has faith with that knowledge."

"What do you mean?"

Nana said, "It takes faith to know that God has the power to change something in our lives, even if He doesn't. It takes faith to understand His authority, even if you don't agree. Trust is where most of us fall short."

Darcy sat quietly again and reflected. And like a flower slowly opening itself to the light of the sun, she started her surrender to Nana's light. Their conversation expanded to life and God's presence in it. They talked about children and suffering and giving birth to new order. And though Nana never took out her Bible, Darcy had a feeling it was somewhere close-by.

"I had a mother who loved me, once," Darcy finally revealed, hours into their talk.

Nana listened intently as Darcy's story unfolded. Almost three months before the train trip, out of the blue, Darcy had received a letter from a close friend of her birth mother. The letter informed Darcy that her mother was very ill and wanted to see her. After talking with her adoptive parents, who were open and very encouraging, Darcy accepted the invitation.

Darcy learned through additional letters that Lilly, her birth mother, never had other children, though she had remarried about a year after Darcy was removed from her home. Lilly had been diagnosed with cancer only six short months ago and the progression was rapid. Already in stage four, she was not expected to survive the holidays.

Nana inhaled deeply. "Death is nothing to fear," she said to Darcy. "It's only a brilliant corridor to all that earth was intended to be, but failed at. It's one of God's big miracles."

Darcy smiled and continued her story. Throughout her childhood, she had been very matter-of-fact about having been adopted. She often fantasized that her mom was there all the time, living anonymously nearby, watching her grow up and being involved. Her favorite fantasy was that her birth mom was one of her mother's friends.

"I was only her daughter for a short time, but I remember her so clearly. I miss her. There wasn't a time in my life that I didn't wish that she was there with me," Darcy said. "I missed her smile, the way she smelled, her cooking, her patty-cake games, her morning coffee, the glasses that she wore when she read her Bible on her big flowered and plastic-covered couch. I even missed watching her fall asleep with her Bible in her hand. . . ."

As Darcy paused, Nana reached into her bag again. This time she pulled out a bag of barbecue chips, Darcy's favorite. Handing them to Darcy without a break in motion, she quietly turned her head and looked past Darcy and out the window.

"I just wish . . ." Darcy stumbled for the right words. "If

only I'd had more time to watch her, I could have been more
like her and my life would have been—"

This time Nana interrupted. "Your life would have been
different. Not better. Not necessarily worse, but different. Don't
second-guess God's redemption. He fixes even our mistakes to
make everything right. You are who you need to be—exactly—
and despite the interruption of your plans. If you want change,
God will change you. And a funny thing happens when
changes take place from the inside out. The outside starts to
look a whole lot less . . . big."

The train went silent. By now, the sun was just over the
horizon and the small light of dawn was breaking through the
train car. The next stop was Idaho Falls, nearly an hour ahead.

"You know," Nana said, "I say, don't bother trying to
understand everything that has happened in your life. It's too
many pieces and our brains are much too small. Besides all
that, we insult God when we presume we can understand His
plan. Just know that the secret to living is having the understanding that life is only what gives you the opportunity to live.
Living is saying yes to all the moving pieces in God's plan and
participating in what happens next."

"She had the best laugh," Darcy said, remembering her
mother.

Nana pulled Darcy in a little closer to her. "Listen to me.
Life is the essence of love, and love is the soul of life. Just live!
Stop guessing, stop looking back, stop wondering, and just live.
Forgive your mother, push past the world, remove the responsi-
bility you've put on yourself to be angry, and just live."

Nana took Darcy by the hand, placed her hand over
Nana's heart, and prayed for her. Darcy could feel every
word that Nana spoke vibrating in her chest and then moving

through Darcy's hands. And with every word, Darcy's soul awoke a little more.

"God, give this child peace." And Darcy started to cry.

"Father, open her up from her soul." And Darcy began to tremble.

"Cause her to continue to question the world, but to trust in your responses." Then Darcy grabbed Nana around the shoulders and squeezed for dear life.

"And finally, let her know her mom's love for her, and yours. Amen."

Darcy somehow felt that she had been given permission to let go of it all. And so she did. The walls fell, the chains broke, and her mind was freed. Darcy saw the Son, and Nana acknowledged His light.

Gathering herself, Darcy said, "Nobody has ever prayed for me before."

Nana gave her a hug and gently said, "I'm sure some-one has."

The train rambled on, and a few minutes later the screech-ing of the brakes to metal brought the train to a stop. It pulled into the station right on time. It was 5:36 AM, December 5, 2007. Darcy kissed her new friend on the cheek and they parted ways.

Darcy's stepfather met her at the station. He hugged her as if he'd known her all of her life. Haltingly, he broke the news that Lilly had passed away early that morning, but that she had left a small box for Darcy.

The drive to Lilly's home was short. When they arrived, Darcy was amazed by all the people who had gathered and the many smiling faces that received her. She met cousins and aunts and uncles. All had wonderful stories about her mom.

Finally, once everyone had gone, Darcy had the opportunity to sit quietly near the fireplace and open her mother's box. In it was a letter from her mother and photos of all of Darcy's special moments: every birthday, every holiday, every date, her prom, and even her wedding. Each picture had a prayer written on the back. Someone—her mom—*had* been praying for her as she grew.

Darcy struggled through tears to read the letter.

5:36 AM, December 5, 2007
My Dearest Little Darcy,

You are having a wonderful life. You are as beautiful and as special as I always knew you would be. From the day that I laid eyes on your beautiful round face, I knew that God had chosen you for great things. Embrace those things, Darcy. Embrace God. You'll never have a better friend.

Darcy went weak in the knees and struggled to catch her breath. Lifting her head from the letter for a minute to gather herself, she noticed a familiar face in a frame placed on the fireplace mantel.

The letter continued.

I know it is probably hard to do right now, but try to forgive me for not being in your life the way you wanted. But please trust me, I've always been there. I have prayed for you every day of your life and loved you every day of my own. Through God's eyes I have watched you grow, through His mercy you have grown, and by His grace you must now live!

Darcy's legs trembled, her heart raced, and she sobbed.

Remember to live, my darling. Life is the essence of love, and love is the soul of life.

I'll see you again! I love you!
Always,
Mom

As she once did so many years before, Darcy's heart called out, "Mommy!"

Searching the room, her attention was drawn again to the photo on the mantel. She slowly rose from the sofa for a closer look. It was Nana. A small note had been placed under the photo:

Lilly Ashton, our beloved Nana
We'll miss your wit, your wisdom, and your love

It's amazing to see the hand of God moving in our lives. One minute we're thinking we've done something wrong to cause Him to leave us to our lessons, and in the next He's proving that He's never left us. In the midst of all the hard stuff, though, we truly experience miracles. God does provide miraculously for our needs. He brings healing to our bodies. And like Darcy, He gives us safe homes to grow in and mothers who love us . . . even from a distance.

God has faithfully touched our lives with wisdom and mercy and hope for the future. We see Him catering to us even in the smallest areas, like long train rides to freedom, longer truths that lead to Him . . . even favorite foods like barbecue potato chips.

He has done and is doing a good work in our hearts, increasing our faith, our patience, and our love for Him. He is working all things together for our good. And occasionally, He'll even send an angel.

Then, just when you're sure that you know how the story will end, the Holy Spirit steps in and blesses everyone.

15

PERSEVERANCE

YEA, THOUGH I WALK THROUGH THE VALLEY

I finished a book the other day that emphasized God's desire to produce positive outcomes in our lives. Although I was happy to be reminded that God is not limited to any societal law or bound by our carnal condition, the author seemed to gloss over the difficult times. I wonder if our focus on Cinderella-story endings serve the whole man.

Testifying about the goodness of God and how He delivers us from our hardships is a good thing. It encourages us to persevere. But our mountaintop experiences are no more significant to strengthening our souls as the stories grown in the valley. And we should tell them all.

This book, and specifically this chapter, has been written to encourage you in your personal journey with the Lord and through the times in your life you find most challenging. The message herein is that no matter what happens, God has not forgotten about you. No matter how long you've been in a rut or in transition, He knows exactly where you are and He is willing to help you out of it.

We live in trying times. Over the years we've seen sin and destruction increase. Drug addictions and abuse are destroying our families and friends. Child neglect, pornography, murder, and even declining self-esteem are widespread. Modern worship, lightheartedness, and high-level feel-good doctrine have invaded the community of believers while the decaying moral fiber of man and a waning desire for holiness have become more apparent. It seems that no matter where we turn, there are signs of defeat and discouragement. We are brokenhearted and wondering how to make it through. We are crying out to God and feeling like there is nothing left in us.

How is it possible to persevere?

Every day we begin at a crossroads with a choice to make: Will I serve God today no matter what or will I throw in the towel and allow the enemy to have the victory?

Let me offer this: "Blessed is the man who endures temptation; for when he has been approved, he will receive the crown of life which the Lord has promised to those who love Him" (James 1:12 NKJV). This is the stuff to focus on that gives you fire under your feet and keeps you moving through life.

Persevering in the middle of our challenges and not allowing the times to negatively influence what we think about God help us not only to *discover* our strengths, but to *practice* them, even if the only strength we possess at the time is simply enduring the present.

For this is how faith is born.

And this faith—staunch and determined—drives us out of our hiding places, pries us loose from our safest illusions, and calls us to a deeper understanding of God, turning life into living. And this faith, actively living no matter what happens around you, really moves mountains. For faith is knowing that God can push a wheelbarrow on a tightrope across the Grand Canyon, and trust is getting on board as He does.

Job said, "Though He slay me, yet will I trust Him" (Job 13:15 NKJV). Job surrendered to God in the middle of his suffering. Jonah surrendered in the belly of a big fish. Jesus gave it all in the darkness of a garden, and I surrendered to Him on a bed in the center of my madness.

Where are you right now?

I encourage you to start wherever you are with your shoulders erect and your trust in God alone. Walk in authority through these trying times, through seemingly overwhelming giants, through self-esteem issues, through drug addictions, abandonment issues, hospital bills, late mortgage payments, homelessness, mental illness, financial strains, broken relationships—straight through the nevertheless and into the strong arms of Christ!

Say, Yes, Lord, my husband has left me and my children, but nevertheless, my sons will be men of God and my daughters will understand their worth as defined by Jesus Christ. Yes, my home is in foreclosure, but nevertheless, this too shall pass.

Personally, I've lived quite a bit for someone my age. Some of my experiences were so emotionally painful that I felt them physically. They are indelibly etched in my memory and have touched me so deep in my soul that I am forever ruined for the ordinary. But I am persuaded that without them, there would be no self-awareness and no discernment of the nevertheless.

Now, assuming that I've got this about right, I propose that as we journey to the center of ourselves, we learn another dimension of faith that births trust that persuades us to proceed undauntedly past our doubts and through the pain of suffering to God's mercy and into the arms of Jesus Christ, down into the valleys and straight through the nevertheless.

And isn't that more good news? There is light at the end of the tunnel and hope on the other side of your situation. Better still, there is a life of everlasting love when this is over. I think that beyond that, the real vantage point and the real miracle of nevertheless is not deliverance from a situation of suffering but learning to *trust* in God as He gives us the quiet strength to face life just as it is!

This means that sometimes we won't be able to pay the bills on time; nevertheless, God is good. Sometimes children will be born to poverty and addicted parents; nevertheless, He is merciful. Sometimes husbands won't surrender to God, children will leave the church, parents will die, the second doctor's opinion will be worse than the first, and the road will only seem to get longer. . . .

Yet through all of life's living, nevertheless, I have overcome. Nevertheless, Christ lives in me. Nevertheless, in my Father's house are many mansions. Nevertheless, I wear a crown. Nevertheless . . . God.

16

HOW MUCH IS THAT LIFE IN THE BIBLE?

THE PRICE OF GRACE

Oh, to be like one of the faithful leaders in the Bible! In particular, I like Paul and the way he did not detour from following Jesus Christ. I also like Moses and the way he was a strong and steadfast leader; and Jeremiah and the way he loved and was committed to the ministry of healing broken souls. That's how I want to live—consistent in my love for God's people. I want to live a "grace-full" life.

While I still struggle in the application of grace, there was a time when I didn't fully understand what grace even meant. I had trouble letting go of the idea that if I *did* the right things for God then God would *do* the right things for me.

From a human perspective, a reciprocal relationship is always easier to accept. It lets us off the hook of indebtedness.

Just in case I found myself between a rock and a hard place, I would keep a mental list of things to do for my beloved Jesus, updated and handy. I was stubborn in my belief about man's ability to "fall from grace" and our right to covenant with God for favor. This deed-and-reward system of thinking was simple enough, approachable, and didn't challenge my li'l cranium too much—until, of course, one September morning in 2001 cracked it wide open.

Starting that day in the World Trade Center, everything I thought I knew about grace was challenged. My spiritual side flipped out, tipped over my "religion," and crash-landed me into reality and the truth about it. That being the substance of things we hope for—or is that faith? Wait, can it be both?

There it was—unmerited, unearned, and unexpected, amazing grace—the something we all hope for. There it was, the divine knowledge by which God's omniscience, His sovereignty, His completeness and vastness infallibly sees all past, present, and future acts and responds proactively at the point where we most need grace.

Grace, compassion, forgiveness, and love were manifested and delivered to me all at once. What a joy it was to see with my own heart the oversized compassion of the almighty God up close in my own life. What an exquisite gift and peaceful place I was in, receiving a profound revelation and being born again into the truth of what a gift of love looks like.

And as I receive it, I learn to give it to others.

––––––

The story is told about a ten-year-old boy who came to know God's grace up close. Barefooted and shivering in the cold, he was peering into a shoe store when a lady approached.

"My little fellow, why are you looking so earnestly in that window?"

"I was asking God to give me a pair of shoes," the boy answered.

The lady took him by the hand and into the store and asked

the clerk for a basin of water and a towel. After removing her gloves, she knelt down and gently washed and dried the boy's feet. Then she asked the clerk to bring the store's best pair of shoes and a half dozen pairs of socks. After making sure they fit, she purchased them and had the remaining socks wrapped up for the boy. Before leaving, she patted him on the head.

"My little fellow, do you feel more comfortable now?"

The astonished lad caught her hand and in tears he searched her face. He answered her question with a question of his own: "Are you God's wife?"

Perhaps that's the way it is supposed to work. Perhaps God shows His grace to us, expecting that we in turn will show it to others. Maybe more emphasis should be on the giving of grace than on the receiving of it. Perhaps as we move through life, meeting people who are searching and hoping for answers, we should respond with grace, lending a shoulder, a revelation, or even a few dollars.

Too many people think they have to earn grace and then talk about how they've fallen short. "Well, I haven't done everything God's been telling me to do." "I didn't read the Word last night." "I didn't pray hard enough." "I haven't fasted." "I didn't give all I could have given in the offering."

If the truth were told, we could all say those things. But does God's grace depend on our actions? NO! God's love is unconditional; His grace is not based on our performance or lack thereof. There are no boxes to check or varying levels of grace to achieve. Grace is found in the character of God, and residually it becomes a lifestyle we live. His grace opens us to himself in whole new ways, re-creating us.

We are saved by the grace of God, and because of His gift of grace, our hearts are changed, our lives are changed. We become more grace-full as we become grace-filled, both in our doing and in our speech. Yes, God desires to work in and through our lives to accomplish His good work. But it is not only a matter of what we are called to do, it is also who we are called to be. God gives it. We pass it on. Grace shows itself in action.

Someone once said that grace breaks through our darkness. Indeed it does! In fact, I can't imagine what brings a smile to God's heart or glorifies Him as much as when broken ones are uplifted by grace that is shown to them and then they find Him through its strength. Even in places where the best of us would struggle and have our human strengths put to the test, God's divine love reaches in—deeply, completely—and recovers us from every kind of suffering.

Every day, God's grace goes the distance for us and with us— through the worst of situations like Hurricane Katrina, the World Trade Center attacks, the genocide in Africa, and the Asian tsunami, to the remarkable landing of US Airways Flight 1549 on the Hudson River. And if we look a little closer, we see grace burst forth in the ordinariness of everyday living.

My friend Veva has taken on the full-time care of her ninety-four-year-old grandmother. Mother Bolden, as we call her, was a dynamic church speaker in her time and is an amazingly strong woman of God. In her younger years, she had a thundering voice and could beat a tambourine until it broke.

Until a few years ago, Mother Bolden still traveled to other churches delivering the gospel of Jesus Christ and encouraging people through difficult times. So you can imagine how difficult it is for her now to accept help in doing the everyday things we take for granted: sitting, standing, eating, bathing, remembering things and people. But there is Veva, gently reminding Mother Bolden every time she forgets something, carrying her from bed to chair and back again despite her own pain, and reading Scripture out loud so earnestly it's like the first time she herself has heard the Word.

Veva is selfless in her actions, as is grace. And the same grace that Mother Bolden has shown for years has returned to her a hundredfold.

For years we have represented grace as simply something from God that yields us endless blessings from heaven. And the essence of grace, we supposed, was that we are broken and unworthy. However, I humbly suggest to you that perhaps grace is something more amazing still. Perhaps grace, as our Father would have it, is also about our sharing it. Perhaps this love, by means of grace, acts in us and with us and through us and around us to achieve God's perfect work.

And while God is the ultimate reason for all the good we do, He requires from all who have the use of reason to give themselves to one another as well. And this is grace—sufficient for all our needs!

17

THE ISSUE OF BLOOD

PRESSING THROUGH SUFFERING

I was reading my Bible the other night and decided to look again at the fifth chapter of Mark. It's where I go to remind myself that God is the God of second chances and impossible situations. I came across an old favorite: the story about the woman with an issue of blood.

Simply told, a woman suffers a hemorrhaging condition for twelve years. She spends all her time and money looking for a cure, but to no avail. Because of the stigma attached to that particular illness at the time, she is ostracized and undoubtedly becomes lonely and desperate. Then one day Jesus comes to town. Believing that He is her last chance for healing, she risks everything to get to Him. And Jesus, seeing her need and her great faith, heals her.

This story, say, from a thirty-thousand-foot view, is brief, simple, and much like the story of David and Goliath in that it is packed with concise life lessons about faith and bearing our burdens. How-ever, up close, it is a bit more disturbing and speaks to faith on a road much less traveled.

My viewpoint started to change when I actually visualized the woman in the depths of her despair. For the first time I considered the intensity and the enormity of the pain she endured. Think about it. The constant blood loss alone would have made the poor woman weak, anemic, pale, and always tired.

She couldn't work, go for long walks, or even shop in local markets because society considered her dirty; it was believed she would contaminate others. Surely her life was reduced to begging for food from a distance and likely going without human touch for years. Her life was literally draining from her body little by little, day by day. Can you imagine?

Now, I can get a bit emotional when it comes to empathizing with the pain of others. And though I shouldn't, I have a tendency to look for reasons behind suffering in order to explain it. Romans 8:18–19 clearly tells us the suffering we experience in this life is nothing compared to the glory that will be revealed in us when we appear in our full and final glory, but I sat there thirsting for more insights beyond the obvious miracle the woman experienced.

I felt led to reread the story from the woman's perspective, and trust me, the view changes radically when looking out from her soul. I'd like to share her story with you as I see it. This might not fit comfortably with traditional teachings, but perhaps that's a good thing. Jesus told the Pharisees their traditions nullified the Word of God (Matthew 15:6).

As you read of the woman's profound desperation, reflect how it relates to any woundedness in your own life. It could be a lost husband, son, or daughter. It could be an illness, financial problems, unrequited love. Whatever the issue, if at any point during this story her words speak on your behalf, quietly press through and call His name out loud . . . *Jesus.*

Carrying the weariness of a woundedness that's heavy enough to drive you through the crowd, past the disapproving eyes of people, straight through the nevertheless and into the extraordinary touch of Jesus Christ . . . press through.

As you do, watch for a supernatural ending to your pain by the opening up of your soul and a gathering to itself of hope, faith, love, authority, strength, endurance, joy, comfort, peace, and meaning. Expect the mending of your broken heart and life. For He says, "I will put my Spirit in you, and you will live again" (Ezekiel 37:14 NLT).

And so the story goes:

I woke to the sound of a rooster crowing at half-light. In my haziness, I thought I smelled my husband's oils and I forgot where I was for a minute. I was two seconds away from delight when the sight of the dirt floor brought me back to reality.

I was still alone in my small, dank room, where I had spent the last twelve years of my life. The room itself would not have been so bad were it not for the loneliness. Sometimes I feel invisible. *Jesus.*

I got out of bed quickly. Needing to get to the well before the townspeople began to gather, I moved about without hesitation, and gathering all of my dirty, bloodstained cloths from the previous day, I stuffed my cloth sack to almost bursting at the seams. So much to carry. *Jesus.*

My walk through town was like a walk through a gauntlet. I hated it. The other women stared and sneered and made cruel remarks. The children laughed at me, pointed, and sometimes they even threw rocks. How can they be so cruel so early in life? What did I do to deserve this fate? What could I have done differently to experience God's favor?

"God, I'm so tired." *Jesus.* "God, I'm so broken." *Jesus.*

There was never anyone else at the well when I would arrive. I wouldn't dare be caught there. I quickly dumped the cloths in the washing trough beneath the flowing waterspouts and scrubbed them. I scrubbed with intent. I scrubbed like there was no tomorrow. I scrubbed like my life depended on it. Sometimes it did.

When I returned home, I stayed there all day.

But it hadn't always been this way. I had a family once: a husband, children, and a good living. Like you, I looked forward to living to a ripe old age with grandchildren, great-grandchildren, and a pretty shawl for my shoulders. But then the bleeding started.

At first it was just irregular and I thought nothing of it. One month it would come and the next month it wouldn't. Sometimes it would be long and other times hardly anything at all. Then one month it flowed and it didn't stop.

Days, weeks, months, and years of doctors and wives' tales and remedies and simple fixes became even more years of depression, feelings of worthlessness, and loneliness. I became the dirty woman by reputation. It was like living in a silo between life and death, without having the permission or the power to just die. *Jesus.*

Meanwhile, the marketplace was abuzz with rumors that a rabbi called Yeshua of Nazareth was coming to the area. People were so excited about Him. They said He had great power. He healed hundreds, gave sight to the blind, opened deaf ears, and restored joy.

Restoration. Restoration. Restoration. What must that be like. . . .

Could I? Is it possible?

As I thought about the possibility of seeing Him, something deep in my gut leaped for joy. I knew I had to go to Him. I had to go to the town square. Somehow I knew He was my last chance. I had to get to Him . . . this Jesus. I had to just speak to Him. But what if I'm heard? If I could just be near Him. But what if I'm caught?

If I could but touch . . . the hem of His garment. But what if they see me? *Jesus.*

It was the break of day. The heat was insufferable. My blood was already flowing heavily, and the stench of it was starting to escape from beneath my dress. My stomach ached. Fear came over me. I pressed on. I wanted to turn back, but I pressed on.

Just as I made it to the edge of town, I saw people pushing toward the square. There were hundreds there. How would I know Him from the others? Would there be a glow or something? What does a Messiah look like?

I followed the crowd, making sure my veil was securely in place. I couldn't afford to be recognized. Just then, I saw a man. My eyes danced at the subtle beauty and grace of Him. He was positively beautiful. Oh my . . . it had to be Him.

He strolled through the crowd almost effortlessly as people screamed and shouted and even fainted at His feet. What manner of man is this? He was polite and gentle, and He went about touching people, praying for them as He walked, holding their faces within His hands and whispering to them. He kissed the children, even hugged the men. Oh my . . . how beautiful He is.

I pushed toward Him through the crowd and close to the ground so no one would notice me. Then I crawled. I literally crawled as people stepped over me, tripped at my back, stepped on my fingers, and kicked me in the head. They never even looked down.

Still I pressed on. I had everything to lose yet everything to gain.

And so I crawled toward Him, and with every muscle in my body tense and deliberate I said His name in a whisper: *Jesus.*

Fill my cup, Lord.

Jesus. Take away the pain, Lord.

The loneliness . . . the depression . . . the agony. *Jesus.*

Imagine being where she was—so close and yet so far. Imagine being on your hands and knees before the Lord God and still feeling invisible. Imagine being so broken and unsure of yourself that even as you lie at the feet of the Master with your heart in bits and strewn before Him, you quiver. Still you know that all that stands between hope and resurrection is a finger's reach.

What would you do?

I know what she did. She pressed. She reached. She touched. *She stopped bleeding.*

The Bible says that immediately after she touched Jesus, the bleeding stopped and He turned and asked who had touched Him. One of his disciples, though the Bible doesn't say which, asked, "Rabbi, what do you mean, who touched you? Look at all these people pressing in on us; many have touched you."

"No," Yeshua insisted. "Someone *touched* me. I felt power leave me."

Now picture this: Jesus knew exactly what had happened. He

knew exactly who had touched Him, why she had touched Him, and where she was when her faith joined her flesh and broke the curse.

To allow onlookers to understand all that was happening, I imagine He turned slowly in the woman's direction. His beautiful eyes might have scanned the crowd, but knowing exactly where she was, He looked down, smiled at her, and reached out to help her to her feet. As she rose, He said, "Daughter, your faith has healed you. Fear not, and go in peace."

But after so many years of suffering and loneliness, living every day without human touch, what she heard probably sounded more like, "It's okay, little one. I'm here now and all is well."

The story ends there, but I imagine the woman remembered His smile for the rest of her life. I imagine she returned to her children and they enjoyed a joyous celebration of the extraordinary in her life.

And so now, what was the reason for the woman's suffering, you ask? Why was she tormented for twelve long years? Why was her story so sad and heartbreaking? Why did she have to carry such a heavy load? She did it for me and you. She did it so that thousands of years later, millions of people might know that the touch of Jesus Christ is bigger than any issue and every power of man. The mere presence of Jesus the Christ changes everything.

And finally, I think she suffered so that we might be reminded that sometimes our sufferings are not unto ourselves, but that others would come to see God. And they do!

I don't know about you, but that makes suffering a bit more okay for me. It lightens the load and changes things. It takes the focus off of Leslie's world and puts it where it should be—on the needs of a lost and searching world. What a privilege it is, then, to suffer so that others might come to Christ.

And so, friends, consider this: Perhaps your struggle is part of a much bigger picture. Does that make things hurt any less? Of course not, but it does make it all worth it. Peter says it is a gracious thing to suffer and to endure—for this is our calling in Christ (1 Peter 2:20–21).

You see, Christ's suffering was for propitiation, ours is for propagation. That is to say, Christ suffered to accomplish salvation and we suffer to spread it.

Finally, let me propose that just maybe the ultimate lesson of the woman's story is not so much about a faith that brings healing to be had by all, but it presents a lesson in radical faith: having enough faith to trust God's bigger purpose, willingly enduring hardship for the good of others in order to provide a clearer view of the only purpose that makes sense—salvation.

"Amazing grace, how sweet the sound, that saved a wretch like me. . . ."

18

A Life Less Ordinary

Expect the Unexpected

I hope one day my life reflects the good graces of our Lord Jesus Christ and that I have risen above life's mediocrity. I hope to somehow conquer a world or two, walk in complete surrender, and live always in the presence of the Lord—breathing, knowing, and experiencing Him every minute.

Today, however, I'm still in the fight. I'm still riding the ups and the downs of my circumstances and choking back the sometimes-life-is-too-hard thumb in my mouth. And as much as I would like for it not to be true, I sometimes want to trade my life of service for the simple and the ordinary.

I love coming home (especially after a long trip) to a comfy bed and a hot bath, to my own desk's clutter, my old worn slippers, and a kitchen that is best when filled with the smell of homemade banana puddin'.

These are the things that put me back in my own skin before I'm forced to face the overwhelming things: the bills, ministry pressures, personal commitments, teenagers, and all the other stuff that shakes my confidence and rips me from my comfort zone.

Surely you must experience this yourself. There is a lot to be said for living a life with little to no interruption. It's nice sometimes to get off the ride and gather yourself. And we'd undoubtedly be a lot more peaceful during the day and relaxed at night. But what would we miss?

How much would you honestly enjoy a heart that never skips a beat, or eyes that never shed tears, lips that never kiss, or a voice that never experiences laughter?

These things are the flavor of life. Yet at the same time most of us want our lives to be simple, expected, and controlled. We want to work hard, marry young, have lots of children, and live in a quiet suburban home with a picket fence until a ripe old age, in a predictable hum of no interruptions.

Snooze on.

But I don't think God is especially interested in quiet hums. Having lived His will, I think He wants us to jump in that wheelbarrow and ride!

Proof of this is seen throughout the Bible. We see God asking His people to step outside of themselves and trust Him for extraordinary adventures. We see Mary's ordinary life interrupted by a messenger of God who impregnated her with the Messiah. Noah was raising his family in a quiet village before his call to build an ark, and Jonah was interrupted with a visit to the inner workings of a big fish.

Nobody expected anything. And though they were all willing to serve the Lord, they had no idea to what extent He would call them.

There is almost no end to biblical examples of the extraordinary. In 2 Kings 6, we read about a floating axhead, and in Joshua 10, the sun stood still. We learn about Deborah, who hadn't planned to lead an army; Moses, who was given up by his mother; Lazarus, who took the trip of a lifetime; and my buddy Paul, who I'm sure was not expecting to write so much of the greatest love story ever told. For him, it started with just one letter.

That's right, one letter. One acceptance of God's invitation to ride and suddenly life is happening in a wheelbarrow. None of these people could see the unexpected ahead in their daily level of existence. Yet all of a sudden there it was! And . . . here it is for us!

You see, when we live for Christ, He calls us to the unexpected—shaking things up, getting the blood flowing, the heart skipping, and the mind fully engaged, until life politely removes itself from the mundane and becomes spectacular.

We are here to encourage others in their journeys, lead people to the Lord, and proclaim a message of hope to those who do not know God. And how can this be done from our rockers? God wants us to get out there, do something, be something, take chances. He tells us to go into all the world (Mark 16:15), build an orphanage, feed the homeless, start a mission, open a shelter, start a street ministry, do something bigger than we ever expected. Mediocrity is easy to achieve. But spectacular, now that takes work!

Going through each day spiritually, mentally, intellectually, and emotionally engaged with a Christ-fixed focus is what I call life. Truly living means we embrace with a wholehearted zest the thrill of everything that is included in life. It's about taking full charge of the moment, giving in to the transformation that changes us from dreamers to doers.

Life is about expecting the unexpected. Living is welcoming blind turns and trusting there is no such thing as coincidences, because God cares too much to leave something as important as eternity to a "what if." Living is all that and then some.

My cousin Ronnie keeps telling me that life always interferes with his leisure. And honestly, I'm glad it does, because personally, I'm more than intrigued by the many brilliantly moving pieces that stretch me beyond this constrictive flesh. And as much as I would prefer to resist the many, many changes in my own life, honestly, the bumpier and more unpredictable the ride, the more I enjoy it.

I don't think we can reap the ultimate reward here or in the everlasting unless we really open ourselves up to all the possibilities that real living offers. And it always comes back to this bottom line: Either you trust God or you don't. Either you believe His Word and His plan for your life or you fight it.

Suppose for a moment what would happen if you were totally convinced that God's love for you is, in fact, as infinite, eternal, and unchangeable as the Bible says it is. Would you give yourself to Him completely by jumping into life and enjoying the great adventure?

They say life is short, but what would it take for you to believe it and then to live like it?

My friend Sujon Low was joking with me one Friday afternoon. We talked about Barack Obama's presidential candidacy and how history was being made simply with his nomination. Sujon went on to declare that Obama would be the new president of the United States. At the time, I was too afraid to hope for so much. It seemed like a fairy tale prediction, so I replied, "Oh, Henny Penny."

Later that night, as I was leaving for the weekend, Sujon teased, "Good night, Leslie. Be careful of falling skies."

Monday morning began like every normal day, except for one thing: Two minutes into my chair, I got the news that Sujon had passed from this life. His heart had just stopped beating the night before. There was no trauma, no pain, and no illness. Sujon had a peaceful and quiet transition into eternity.

The thing is, though I miss him, I don't feel sad for Sujon. I rejoice in where he is right now and in the wonderful experience he is now having. I can't wait to be there too! His death, however, is a huge reminder of how quickly life can change. All of us are just a heartbeat away from crisis, transition, and extraordinary things.

And though I think God has placed a desire in our hearts to live life's complete adventure, a lack of faith keeps us on the platform. We fear we won't be able to fulfill God's plan for us or some horrible consequences might unfold. We think people will point and say mean things if we live outside the box. And so we settle for the ordinary. But the problem with living this way is that it settles us into complacency and we lose our dreams, our visions, and our faith in God's impossible. It hides our eyes from the wondrous possibilities and diminishes great expectations. Without expectancy, there is nothing to look forward to and nothing to propel us into greatness.

———

I'm not a surfer, but I understand a little about how it's done. The surfer steadies him or herself on the board by keeping a low center of gravity. With knees slightly bent, feet firmly planted, head facing forward, shoulders strong, and arms out to the side for balance, he rides the waves.

The surfer has to be braced for the next inevitable wave. Then he or she just rides it. Of course, the challenge comes in staying on the board, riding, not fighting the tide, and keeping a forward-facing focus. That's because the body (and board) will naturally follow the focus.

How cool is that? Your body will follow your focus. Wherever the surfer's eyes are directed, the board will follow. So no matter how big or small the wave, if he is positioned correctly and focused, he'll keep his head above water.

Isn't that just like living? Don't you think that if we just brace ourselves for the next inevitable wave, keeping our eyes on the prize—heaven, our eternal home—life will become a big adventure as opposed to a big ol' giant?

I've said it before and I'll say it again: Life is an all-encompassing journey! Living life to its fullest, embracing its challenges, bracing ourselves, and then waiting with great expectancy for some wonderful and brilliant thing to shake us up or take us by surprise *is* the journey. I love it and wouldn't have it any other way.

Life should be dramatic! It should be unpredictable! It should not be something we simply survive, fearful of what could happen next. When all is done, we should have unbelievable life stories, each borne from our unique experiences and God-given individuality.

Just imagine the stories, the songs, and the smiles when we arrive at heaven's gates.

My brother Leonard is a wonderful guy. He's always polite, always pleasant, and even when he's upset, he doesn't raise his voice. When he gets to heaven, I think he'll walk around shaking hands with everyone he sees, politely thanking them for inviting him in. He'll likely be wearing a button-down shirt and khaki Dockers.

My sister Lanette will stop, pose for the camera, and then break into a solo. My mother probably arrived singing and doing a holy dance with her left arm swinging in the air. My cousin Ronnie is going to walk in lifting weights, trying his best to make going to heaven a masculine kind of thing. My sister Lenore will probably just giggle her way in.

And me, I'll get there all right . . . but I'll be breathing hard, my hair will be all over the place, my knees will be scraped, my clothes will be a little torn, and I'll be sliding in like I'm stealing home plate. The angel Gabriel will have to help me up off the floor, and as he does, I'll be dusting myself off, looking around in excitement and saying, "Wow! What a ride!"

19

THE PLANS I'VE MADE

OH, REALLY?

Walk down our streets day or night. Beneath the sounds of everyday living, you will find people with deep, deep wounds. And if you really listen, you can hear them weeping.

Go on, lean in. Hear a nation full of amazing people, humbled greatness, wellsprings of creativity, who are angry, despised, confused, depressed, and licking their wounds. These are the beautiful souls of the common man—real people—trapped behind walls of rejection and believing they are alone and unloved.

And so they suffer. Drowning in a vista of poverty, prostrating themselves and crying out in desperation to the only God of hope . . . that He would hear and deliver them.

They sleep in places we can't imagine. They eat things that would turn the stomach of the average man, and yet they survive by the mercy of God. From this tomb of desperation they hold on to the only thing that keeps them alive—a love for God and a faith in Him that is unmatched by anything we've ever known.

And then they dream, constructing images of great and seemingly unbelievable things to summon up time and time again strength enough just to live. Left to only imagine what parallel worlds exist under the same blue skies and cotton clouds that others take for granted every day, they survive in every state, every city, and every skid row in this world. These are the broken ones.

I once believed that desperation bred despondency. But then I met the crooked man who walked the crooked mile. He was broken down, dirty, and wide-eyed. His back was bent from wear and tear, his shoes were worn, and his clothes hung from his body. He smelled of smoke and like he'd been sleeping in a sewer. With his index fingers and thumbs, he made a triangle in front of his mouth and began to speak out.

All around him was chaos. Every inch of this mile was packed with hundreds of roaming people: no teeth, dirty, fighting, cussing at the cosmos, walking into traffic, lying in corners, picking through garbage and carts, and just being. Blanketed with the cruelty of their addictions and fears, they hung on to life by a thread.

Still, he stood trembling in the midst of it all preaching his message: "Be strong and courageous." His eyes watered and his voice trembled as he struggled through his message to the hundreds. Within seconds, his soft words became more passionate with each syllable . . . lyrical, rhythmic. I couldn't tell if he was singing or speaking. Then I recognized its rhythm. "I-I-I heard somebody say . . . God won't leave us here."

The tenor vibrato of his voice made it impossible for passersby to keep moving. They stopped and listened with me. And as the words flowed with even more conviction, his voice got raspier. His eyes opened wider and his fists clenched.

Some people watched in disbelief, while others, offended, walked away. I took it all in, imagining what he must have been like as a child. What were his dreams, and where did life go left when it should have gone right . . . delivering him to "down-and-out" and grabbing for hope on a busy corner of skid row?

Then, as if more determined to get his message across and perhaps to believe it himself, he screamed at the top of his now-strained voice, "God loves us!" And the passion of his future hopes barreled through his homelessness, past his despair and straight through the nevertheless. I felt his heart through my own and I believed him.

So now, believe me when I tell you that desperation yields hope! I'm convinced that somewhere in us is the God-placed urge to hope—a hope that is hard won, grounded, and resolute in every situation and despite the odds. For this is the hope that grows us up through our crises and keeps us wanting, moving about, stirring, getting up in the morning, going to bed at night, and living.

———

It's Saturday night. I'm on Michigan Avenue in Chicago, eating at an outdoor café. The weather is amazing, and I am caught up in the beauty of the evening sky. To my left, a woman in a crisp off-white linen suit quietly sips her chilled espresso. To my right, a homeless man approaches with a small child who looks to be under the age of eight. Together they check the tables around me for leftovers.

"When I grow up, I want to be homeless with my daughter and teach her self-worth from a park bench in the city."

It's Friday evening. I'm leaving a speaking engagement in London that has attracted more than twenty-eight hundred people. As I leave the auditorium a woman approaches me in tears. She gently brings my face closer to hers and transfers her pain through my ear.

"When I grow up, I want to suffer through loneliness and suicidal tendencies."

It's any day of the week, any place in the world, and someone is disappointed because things aren't quite the way they should be. Something else has gone wrong.

"When I grow up, I want to stay in the fire, so that my faith in God is constantly tested."

Nobody says, "When I grow up, I want to be addicted to drugs or strung out in poverty." Nobody dreams of being abused, raped, or embittered. No one prays to lose their children to the streets or their parents to premature death. We don't ask for cancer, AIDS, or PTSD (post-traumatic stress disorder). Nobody wants to be unhappy.

All of us have plans for our lives. Beginning with the childhood infinitude of shooting rubber bands at the moon, building castles in the sky, and enjoying the fantasies only a child can see, we planned to have the complete American dream. We planned to become astronauts and firefighters and basketball players and doctors and nurses and teachers and moms and dads. We wished for happy family times in joy-filled homes.

These were the plans we made. We didn't imagine we would lose our jobs, or our marriages, or our homes. But sometimes this is life, and life is what happens in the middle of all our plans.

But take heart, my friends, there is good news! "I know the plans I have for you," declares the Lord, "plans to prosper you and not to harm you, plans to give you hope and a future" (Jeremiah 29:11). The word *prosper* can be translated as *shalom*, or *peace*. Other Bible translations say God has plans for our "welfare" or our "wholeness."

In His vastness, the Lord has designed a unique plan to restore hope to our lives. And the prosperity He intends for us extends beyond the temporal and into eternity with Him. No matter the situation, everything always, always, always comes back to the bottom line of God's bigger picture: His redemption plan to restore us to himself.

Even though we may have to eat the bitter fruit of our self-willed ways, God has good plans for each of us . . . spiritual wellness. Choice by choice and revelation by revelation, He gently moves us into a heart-centered life of peace, wholeness, and hope. As we follow God's guidance and open our hearts to Him, we move closer to our appointed end.

What's more important than that? Can you honestly say that when you get to glory and see the Lord face to face that the topic of your conversation will be what happened here on earth?

When you are kicked back and easy in the beauty of the heavens, living everything a hundred times better than you ever imagined; when the shores are pushing the sands back and forth around your feet while the laughter of friends and family can be heard for miles; when our Lord God is walking through the gardens calling your name . . . what could be better?

20

HIS PLANS, HIS VISION

WHAT "PERFECT" LOOKS LIKE

When I was a little girl, I believed in magic. In fact, I was starry-eyed about most everything. I blew fluffy dandelion seeds into the wind, wished on stars, threw pennies into fountains, and constantly searched for four-leaf clovers. In particular, though, I liked fairies. I checked for them every night and paused at thresholds to watch for them in the "in-betweens." I remember placing a small jeweled box that my grandmother had given me underneath my bed so the fairies could make their home. Day after day, I believed they were real and would make my dreams come true.

My mother was a practical woman. Although she encouraged our visions, she was not a big fan of fairy tales and make-believe. She'd much rather be sitting us down going over the economics of our household than encouraging fantasy. And yet despite her words to me that fairies were not real, I kept wishing every night. I kept hoping every day. I kept dreaming over and over again.

Then it happened. I was cleaning my room one day and sweeping under my bed when I felt the broom move something against the wall. It wasn't heavy, but it was resistant. Out of curiosity, I peeked under the bed but couldn't see anything. I pushed and swept in the opposite direction until the object finally revealed itself. It was my jeweled box from years before, dusty but solid, beautiful but still empty.

I picked it up and sat in the corner. Holding that box again, I remembered all the holidays and birthdays and Christmas mornings and other great days it had kept me looking forward to. And for the life of me, I couldn't figure out when I had grown up and stopped checking for fairies.

I laugh at myself today, but in hindsight there's a lesson here. Looking for magic keeps us facing forward as we grow up, but perhaps the magic is that we do grow up. Our priorities change. Our dreams become visions and we plan for them. Our desires shift gears, we subscribe to a bigger picture, and perspectives become matters of fact. God-yielded wills bring God-planned lives.

I never planned to be who I am today, but I couldn't have made a better choice! As the Lord is peeling back the layers of the Leslie I created to reveal the Leslie of His intent, I find that I like who I am in Christ.

Like everyone else, I'm on the path of forever-learning. I stubbornly hang on to a few old ways and ideas, and from time to time I kick and scream into His future, but I go forward. I'm working hard on immediately obeying His tugging lest the desires of my flesh become my plans and motivation, and the substandards set by this world persuade me to lower my own. Lest worldly power and corporate ambition darken my soul and deafen my ears to the voice of God until the god of this world becomes my lead and I am blinded to the vision of the Leslie whom God is unfolding before me. Lest I lose sight of the big picture.

I heard a story about the man who drew up the engineering plans for the Brooklyn Bridge. During its construction, he was injured. For months he was shut up in his room and could not work. He communicated with the workmen through his wife, who every day carried the plans and documents to the workers.

After years of planning and construction, the bridge was completed at last. The architect was so excited he couldn't bear to stay away. He asked several friends to carry him to the bridge on a cot and place him where he could see the entire structure.

There he lay, intently scanning the work of his genius: the great cables, the massive piers, the mighty anchorages that fettered the bridge to the earth. His critical eye ran over every beam, every girder, every cord, every rod, every detail. As the joy of the achievement filled his soul, he shouted, "It's just like the plan! It's just like the plan!"

I love this story, because I love when a plan comes together. When after suffering and working and praying God does His thing and you see it with your own eyes, there is nothing better! It is good news! God has designed the perfect plan for our lives and is presently pulling together all the necessary pieces to complete His perfect work (James 1:4).

The artist Michelangelo was known to choose huge, shapeless blocks of marble to create his masterpieces. When asked why, he responded, "I saw the angel in the marble and I carved until I set him free." Similar to Michelangelo, God saw us in the stars, and He lovingly and gently carved in the earth until He formed us. He continues today molding and making us into the "us" of His vision. We need only to stay pliable, perhaps okay with sometimes being out of work longer than we'd hoped, or changing directions after ten years of going a certain way, or deciding to love someone who is not the picture of the mate we envisioned.

God's plan might not necessarily lift us out from our present surroundings, because it is not a new sphere God is seeking. It is a new man in the present sphere! And when one gives over his own will and receives God's perfect plan, God will grow him where he's been planted.

In the twenty-ninth chapter of Jeremiah, God is talking to the elders and priests who were in exile. He tells them to pray, and assures them He is with them. The eleventh verse, which we discussed in the previous chapter, is where God declares that He knows His plans for our lives.

But wait, here's the part that's usually overlooked. The tenth verse reads, "This is what the Lord says: 'When seventy years are completed for Babylon, I will come to you and fulfill my gracious promise to bring you back to this place.' " In other words, when this is over, it will be all right.

God's plan is to prosper us spiritually, according to His perfect will and purpose. His plan is to give us enough hope to press through any suffering and into a future with Him. He builds us up in His Word, using all the right people, gifts, circumstances, and yes, even things designed for our demise, to bring us back to Him. God-yielded wills bring God-planned lives.

My pastor was teaching about the Great Commission and impressed upon us the idea of spreading the Good News "as we are going." He emphasized living the entire moment for God, and then doing the next thing: Sing the song, teach the class, visit the sick, prepare the meals on wheels, befriend the homeless, and spread the Good News.

And so as we go, God's breath gives new life in Christ, creating possibilities in us and transforming our lives from the inside out.

For me, all of my experiences make life juicy and worthwhile. Traveling, good food, live music, and giving to others all rank much higher than all the stuff I used to collect and plan for. Yes, I have hopes and goals and things I would like to have. In fact, there are a few remaining tasks on my project plan, but I'm not married to the timeline or the outcome.

You see, when you exchange your plans for the Lord's, you start to see life through His looking glass. With this perspective, you can't help but shout, "It's just like the plan! It's just like the plan!"

21

HIS PROMISES

A FEW OF MY FAVORITE THINGS

"Let God's promises shine on your problems." ~Corrie ten Boom

"Promise only what you can deliver. Then deliver more than you promise." ~Author unknown

"God's promises are like the stars; the darker the night the brighter they shine." ~David Nicholas

My father was a promise keeper. He said what he meant and he meant what he said—all the time. He was very intentional in his communication, so if he gave you his word, you could count on it.

I'm remembering one time in particular when I was about eleven years old. My brother Leon and I wanted another dog. We already had a small French poodle, but she was hardly the kind we wanted.

We wanted one that we could make chase our friends and scare our enemies. We wanted *fierce*.

Well, long story short: Mom said no new dog, and Dad quietly said, "I'll get ya one." Even though Mom talked louder than Dad and was really good at getting him to change his mind, Leon and I believed Dad. A year later we had a brown German shorthair puppy named Penny.

My brothers, sisters, and I learned faith from our mother and trust from our dad. Knowing that he would do what he said he'd do made us feel secure. It also went a long way in teaching us about boundaries.

Today, it's my heavenly Father's words that keep me secure. I know I can count on His Word without doubt. Even when I pray about something and wait longer than I'd like, I trust He will supply my true needs, not only the physical ones.

All of His promises are rich and full, governing every area of my life, ensuring my wholeness and a successful completion to my journey. I count on them.

Often in my travels I'm asked to share my favorite Scriptures. I'd like to say the entire sum of the Bible is my favorite. But a few verses do stand out in my life and help me in my personal challenges. My prayer is that they will bless your heart as they do mine.

A Few of My Favorite Things

• *When I'm feeling challenged and out of sorts.*

I am the Lord, the God of all mankind. Is anything too hard for me? — Jeremiah 32:27 niv

• *These days most everything is so complex. I think people are looking for simplicity. I remember these Scriptures when I'm talking about God saving us and our loved ones.*

So they said, "Believe on the Lord Jesus Christ, and you will be saved, you and your household." – Acts 16:31 NKJV

If my people, who are called by my name, will humble themselves and pray and seek my face and turn from their wicked ways, then will I hear from heaven and will forgive their sin and will heal their land. – 2 Chronicles 7:14

"Though the mountains be shaken and the hills be removed, yet my unfailing love for you will not be shaken nor my covenant of peace be removed," says the Lord, who has compassion on you. – Isaiah 54:10

• *When I'm feeling a little afraid of doing the next thing in God's plans, I think of these:*

Be strong and courageous. Do not be afraid or terrified because of them, for the Lord your God goes with you; he will never leave you nor forsake you. . . . The Lord himself goes before you and will be with you; he will never leave you nor forsake you. Do not be afraid; do not be discouraged. – Deuteronomy 31:6, 8

In my distress I called to the Lord; I called out to my God. From his temple he heard my voice; my cry came to his ears. – 2 Samuel 22:7

But you are a shield around me, O Lord; you bestow glory on me
    and lift up my head.
To the Lord I cry aloud, and he answers me from his holy hill.
I lie down and sleep; I wake again, because the Lord sustains me.

I will not fear the tens of thousands drawn up against me on every
side. – PSALM 3:3–6

The Lord is my shepherd;
I shall not want.
He makes me to lie down in green pastures;
He leads me beside the still waters.
He restores my soul;
He leads me in the paths of righteousness
For his name's sake.
Yea, though I walk through the valley of the shadow of death,
I will fear no evil;
For you are with me;
Your rod and your staff, they comfort me.
You prepare a table before me in the presence of my enemies.
You anoint my head with oil;
My cup runs over.
Surely goodness and mercy shall follow me
All the days of my life;
And I will dwell in the house of the Lord
Forever. – PSALM 23 NKJV

• *Sometimes I can be a bit impatient and my inclination is to kick doors*
open rather than wait for the Lord. So when I'm getting a little tired
of waiting on God to do something and I need to encourage myself to
be still, I think of Psalm 42:11:

Why are you cast down, O my soul? And why are you disquieted
within me? Hope in God; for I shall yet praise Him, the help of
my countenance and my God. – NKJV

• *When I'm feeling a bit sorry for myself about loss and struggling to keep my focus on the treasures that wait for me in heaven, I think of:*

Let not your heart be troubled; you believe in God, believe also in Me. In My Father's house are many mansions; if it were not so, I would have told you. I go to prepare a place for you. And if I go and prepare a place for you, I will come again and receive you to Myself; that where I am, there you may be also. – John 14: 1–3 NKJV

I will lift up my eyes to the hills;
From where does my help come?
My help comes from the Lord,
Who made heaven and earth.
He will not let your foot be moved;
He who keeps you will not slumber. – Psalm 121:1–3 ESV

• *When I want nothing more than to be immediately obedient to God, but His plan—what He is doing in my life or the lives of those around me—doesn't make sense to my eyes and my flesh is threatening to put Leslie back in charge of my decisions…*

Trust in the Lord with all your heart and lean not on your own understanding; in all your ways acknowledge him, and he will make your paths straight. – Proverbs 3:5–6

But those who wait on the Lord shall renew their strength;
They shall mount up with wings like eagles
They shall run and not be weary,
They shall walk and not faint. – Isaiah 40:31 NKJV

- *When the enemy of my soul is fighting my son, invading my thoughts, and from the surface it doesn't look very good:*

But thus says the Lord: "Even the captives of the mighty shall be taken away,
And the prey of the terrible be delivered; for I will contend with him who contends with you,
And I will save your children." – Isaiah 49:25 NKJV

- *When I want to reflect on the holiness of God:*

In the year that King Uzziah died, I saw the Lord sitting on a throne, high and lifted up, and the train of His robe filled the temple. Above it stood seraphim; each one had six wings: with two he covered his face, with two he covered his feet, and with two he flew. And one cried to another and said:

"Holy, holy, holy is the Lord of hosts;
The whole earth is full of His glory!"

And the posts of the door were shaken by the voice of him who cried out, and the house was filled with smoke. So I said:

"Woe is me, for I am undone!
Because I am a man of unclean lips,
And I dwell in the midst of a people of unclean lips;
For my eyes have seen the King,
The Lord of hosts."

Then one of the seraphim flew to me, having in his hand a live coal which he had taken with the tongs from the altar. And he touched my mouth with it, and said:

"Behold, this has touched your lips;
your guilt is taken away,
and your sin purged." – Isaiah 6:1–7 NKJV

• *When I want to remind myself of my surrender to the ministry of Jesus Christ:*

Also I heard the voice of the Lord, saying:
"Whom shall I send,
And who will go for Us?"
Then I said, "Here am I! Send me." – Isaiah 6:8 NKJV

Father, your Word brings life. Let it be to me as you have said. Amen.

WE "MADE" THIS WORLD

NOW WE LIVE IN IT

Once, at the beginning of time, God created Adam and Eve, placed them in a garden, and told them to take care of the land (Genesis 2:15). It was God's original plan that Adam and Eve would live all their days in the presence of a loving Father. He would fellowship with them and they would return His love, be fruitful, and multiply.

In God's plan, each generation would grow up in the light of His love, without ever knowing a day of rejection or pain.

Then one day, as Adam stood by, an enemy stole into the garden and deceived Eve, challenging God's Word and tempting her to disobey God. The enemy said to the woman, "You will not surely die" (Genesis 3:4). In other words, surely God is a liar.

Eve believed the enemy and convinced Adam to join her in her disobedience. Together their actions called God a liar and brought death into the world. Soon after their fatal error, God, knowing exactly what had happened, walked in the garden and called to the man, "Where are you?"

Adam told God that he was afraid because he was naked, so he hid himself. He ran behind a bush, but it was not tall enough. He ran to the trees, but they were not wide enough. So using the intelligence that God had gifted to him, he made a protective covering, first of fig leaves. Later that "covering" would be pyramids, buildings, and then skyscrapers.

And again God called to Adam, but Adam ran from God. God sent a Messiah to redeem Adam and his race. But Adam ignored the call. Instead he ran farther and faster. Using the skills God had given him, he would later construct automobiles, planes, and trains to move him throughout the Earth and further away from God.

And Adam grew in self-indulgence and forged his own agenda. Using plans and strategies to construct a new world, he increased his possessions but diminished his values. He formed more groups but was less organized. Adam lost sight of God's provision and trusted his possessions. He made plans with no paths, celebrated answers with no meaning, paid less attention to God but talked more about Him. He had great knowledge but he was left wanting. Then Adam distorted God's vision and lost sight of himself.

And God called.

And God, knowing exactly what had happened, reached out again to the man. "Adam," He said, "where are you?"

But Adam did not answer. Instead, he buried himself in justification. He formed weapons and tools of destruction and posed wars against himself that he could not win. And using the authority that God had gifted him with, he suffocated his spirit with carnal indulgences and overlooked the price he had to pay.

Adam forged a new path. He used other gods and idols to support his new nature and he defiled his soul. Churches were formed.

And churches broke up. And cults were created and cults broke up. And confusion inhabited the souls of mankind. And so Adam built church buildings to gather in but forgot how to worship. He added years to his life but lacked quality of living. He learned to speak clearer but forgot how to pray. He reached for the stars but would not bend his knee. Adam gained the whole world but lost his own soul.

As knowledge increased, so did the sins of man. And the earth seemed veiled with darkness. There came apostasy and moral disintegration. And there came genocide, homicide, and crimes against humanity. There were child abductions, hunger, and economic decline. There came poverty and hatred, and then brokenness was continental.

And God required repentance of Adam, and Adam blamed God. God had sent a book of letters and a road map by which Adam could return. But Adam lost his way. And so God planned for redemption, His spirit planned for comfort in the journey, and Jesus planned His return.

And now we wait. Enduring a world of confusion and chaos that our decisions have made, trying to overcome the sin nature that binds us to it, we struggle to be free. We're scrambling to remember what it must have been like in a garden of perfection before our desire to be god separated us from God.

And so the primary message of this story is really the backdrop of life: man's choice to reject God and leave the garden, and God's choice to provide for him a way to return. And as we—Adam—travel this road back home, God has made provision for our guidance, our comfort, and our strength. Anticipating our struggles, He has given us grace to endure, hope beyond suffering, and a love that conquers all.

I'm hoping that in your journey, every time you incur hardships they will remind you of a garden that once was and an enemy that seeks to keep you from returning to it. My hope is that we all press toward the mark for the prize of the high calling of God in Christ Jesus (Philippians 3:14). And that we pray for one another and hope for one another, and fight back and talk back (see chapter 24) and believe God again. And recognizing the sound of His voice once more, I pray that we will respond with great joy when He calls again to us, "Where are you?"

23

TAKING UP YOUR CROSS

A CALL TO ARMS

A few years ago I was excited to see the movie *The Passion of the Christ*, which was having a profound impact on Christians and non-Christians alike. When I finally saw it, I was so moved that I immediately started a study on the Crucifixion and the stations of the Cross—the final hours of Christ.

I read about the Crucifixion in the Bible as well as every expository writing on the subject I could find. Halfway through my study, Simon of Cyrene, the man who carried the cross for Jesus, caught my attention. While the Bible doesn't tell us much about him, it does say Simon was pulled out of the crowd to take Christ's cross on his shoulders and bear the weight of His load. What an eternal honor to be known as the one who helped Jesus Christ in His hour of need.

It got me to rethink an old school of thought about hardship and suffering.

All my life I've heard Christians refer to their difficulties or challenges as being their "cross to bear." There's an underlying tone of "if I must, I must," as if bearing a cross is a rite of passage.

My intent here is not to offend. In fact, I say this in all humility: In light of what Simon did, what Jesus taught, and the true association of the cross, the line of reasoning I mention above makes no sense to me. In fact, it's borderline insulting. Consider this: How can being associated with Christ in any way be a burden to bear? How can we take on the attitude "If I must, I must"?

———

And so, I'd like to share Simon's story in a new way. This is not a literal retelling of the Bible account. I imagined it from the perspective of a passerby who might have noticed Simon on his road to transformation.

Try to visualize the streets of Jerusalem at this time in history. Sanitary conditions were at best poor, and since the whole city was filled with people for the Passover celebration, conditions must have been even worse. Filth and debris filled the streets. It was likely hot and crowded, with the crush of people rushing to and fro. They're about to see Jesus, carrying His cross past Simon, whom I refer to as the stranger.

In those days, the townsmen lined the streets to watch the guilty pass through to the place where they would be crucified. It was hot and sticky this day. The sky was overcast and the air was stale and still. There was something noticeably different in the atmosphere.

I have to admit, I was a little curious about the one they

called Christ and so I joined the crowd. Hundreds pushed past me, and though my intent was not to follow but rather to be a casual observer, I had no choice but to move with the flow. We rushed in a panicked hurry.

Then another man, tall and strong, looked to be passing through. He walked against the crowd. I could tell he was a stranger to this land, because he carried a large bag across his shoulder and looked somewhat lost. *"A certain man from Cyrene, Simon, the father of Alexander and Rufus, was passing by on his way in from the country"* (Mark 15:21). The road at the beginning of the Via Dolorosa was where I first saw the stranger. He looked tired, sluggish, not at all interested in what was going on around him. He didn't seem at all curious about the man they called Christ, and judging from the way he pushed opposite the crowd, he had no idea where he was going.

This road was about twelve feet wide. Rough and rocky, it led up a straight incline before it sloped toward the Damascus Gate. And then He appeared.

It was Jesus, with the heavy cross on His shoulders. I almost passed out when I saw Him. Blood covered his entire body, so much so that His fingertips looked to be dripping blood. His feet were swollen, He was sweating into His open wounds, and the pace of His walk was staggered. That cross on His shoulders was ragged and splintered and looked to weigh at least three hundred pounds.

People gathered in the streets and on rooftops. Some laughed and others were silent. Some turned their heads and dabbed at their eyes, while others yawned with disinterest. I wanted to hide my face, but I couldn't take my eyes off of Him.

I kept wondering, *Why?* Why would He go through all of this if He truly were the Messiah?

The wind blew ever so slightly and the stench of sewage accosted me. Trying to keep up with the pace of the crowd, I stumbled into a pile of garbage and tripped over two large rats rummaging through it.

Suddenly the crowd was shouting. As I elbowed my way toward the front, I saw Jesus on His knees. He'd fallen. People began yelling obscenities and spitting at Him. Someone even kicked Him.

Then I noticed the stranger again. Still looking out of place and somewhat disoriented, our eyes met. He quickly averted his gaze, trying to be inconspicuous. But a soldier, not willing to be delayed getting to the place called The Skull, seized the stranger and forced him to carry the cross.

Surveying his surroundings, he reluctantly started to help. The fear in his face was obvious; the crowd would no doubt associate him with Jesus and demand his death as well or at least strike out at him.

I think Jesus sensed his concern. He used all of His remaining strength to gather himself and stand next to the stranger, shoulder to shoulder. Sharing the weight of the other side of the crossbeam, Jesus nodded slightly. His lips turn upward, forming a small smile, even a comforting one. How could it be?

The stranger seemed stunned. I wondered what he was thinking. He blinked and then seemed to lose himself in Jesus' loving gesture. The moment was interrupted when an impatient guard pushed them both, forcing them on their way. This time the stranger stood stronger, more erect and resolute. I think I detected a tear on his cheek. Even as the soldiers continued to whip Jesus, He carried the cross, and the stranger became more involved.

At one point, Jesus fell again. In a rage of frustration, Simon drove away the crowd and the soldiers. At another, he tried to hold Jesus up as He stumbled under the weight. Finally they arrived at the place called The Skull. The stranger turned to Jesus and stared for a very long time. Jesus looked back, and the stranger walked away.

I wonder if he cried.

When I completed this story and put down my pencil, I reflected on my own life and discovered a few things. Taking up my cross isn't suffering at all, it is an honor!

As a Christian, we take up our crosses when we choose to follow Christ. Like Simon, we pick them up to walk with Jesus, and with strong shoulders, an upright posture, and a face that dares to confront the crowd, we stand firm in our conviction to be like Him in all that we do: "If we have been united with him like this in his death, we will certainly also be united with him in his resurrection" (Romans 6:5).

One day, we'll enjoy a glorious feast of overcoming with all the saints and the elders and those who have gone before us. One day we will meet face-to-face with the One who saved us, and then at long last, we'll put down our crosses in exchange for the crown of life, presented by the very hand of our Creator, God.

But all this, only if we choose to take up our crosses!

24

As a Man Thinks

Let the Words of My Mouth . . .

I am convinced, after much contemplation, that the mind really is a terrible thing to waste. Unfortunately, our minds are the chosen battleground of our adversary, the devil. He wants to see us forever separated from the Lord. Obviously the stakes are high. We are literally fighting for our lives.

For thousands of years the enemy has studied our behavior and perfected the art of deception. He finds ways to whisper lies to us, causing wrong behavior, wrong thinking, and wrong beliefs. Our entire culture has been saturated with his schemes and subtle to blatant messages everywhere—in movies, advertisements, song lyrics; you name it. His goal is to take our focus off of truth and pull us away from God.

I picture the devil trolling about the earth, especially looking to devour someone on the brink of a God-change or transformation

(1 Peter 5:8). But you can't really blame him; he's just doing what he does.

Our job is to resist the enemy. Our responsibility is to take back control of our mind, search out the truth about God, and then believe it. We decide what we dwell on and what we discard. We either buy into the enemy's lies or we put him under our feet. Because what he offers us is nothing.

My brother Pastor Lawrence Haskin illustrated this truth to me some time ago. He balled up a piece of aluminum foil and handed it to me while we talked. I held it, waiting to hear what I should do with it. In the meantime, with my mind on the foil, I missed some of the conversation. Finally, Lawrence asked why I was holding on to garbage. The ball of foil was of no use to me; it was a distraction, it was garbage. And I just took it because it was given to me. No questions asked or pushing back.

That's exactly what the enemy does to us. He hands us garbage and we take it. No questions asked and no pushing back. We take it. Hold on to it. And get distracted from God's grace happening around us.

Throw the enemy's garbage away! Better still, don't take it. You control your mind. We don't have to pursue every thought that enters our heads.

Every war ever fought began with a thought. Every deed ever done, righteous or unrighteous, was first conceived in the mind. The mind has been, is now, and will remain until our Lord's return the spiritual battleground wherein victory is secured or forfeited, based on the choices we make.

If you resist the devil, he will run away. Yes, he will try to deceive you again, but there are ways to fortify yourself. The Bible tells us not to give place to the devil (Ephesians 4:27). Meaning, don't provide an area of your life where he can be comfortable or establish strongholds that cause you to doubt God or fear life changes desired by God. His Word also says, "Whatever is true, whatever is noble, whatever is right, whatever is pure, whatever is lovely, whatever is admirable—if anything is excellent or praiseworthy—think about such things" (Philippians 4:8).

———

One day I was on my way from where I live in upstate New York to New York City. I had to drive across the Tappan Zee Bridge, one of the larger bridges in New York. Keep in mind that I was diagnosed with PTSD after 9/11, so to put it mildly, my nerves were a bit on edge. Certain activities and smells bring back that day's events in floods and trigger panic in me.

As I approached the bridge, anxiety set in. My hands started to sweat, my heart beat faster, and I felt my usual sense of wanting to flee. Adding to everything, an 18-wheeler was driving next to me. My enemy, the devil, said to me, "You know that truck next to you is carrying explosives for another terrorist attack. The bridge will collapse and you will drown."

At that exact moment, the truck hit a large bump and I went into a full panic attack. I screamed and started to swerve across lanes while cars around me blasted their horns. Then my mind cut in with another thought: "If you drive the car off the bridge you can get away from the truck. You can jump out halfway down and survive."

I actually contemplated it. And I promise you, there was no awareness whatsoever that this would have been suicide. In the midst of this my phone rang and I somehow managed to pick it up. My brother's voice was on the other end.

See what I mean when I say that God is active in our lives?

Lawrence was calling to check on me. I had told him the night before about my plans to visit the city and the fear I anticipated.

After I quickly described my situation, he calmly responded

with something like this: "Leslie, listen to me. Stop thinking what you are thinking and think differently. Think about things that are good, things that are honest, things that are pleasing to the Lord and His truths. Then the peace of God WILL protect you and your MIND from confusion and fear."

I think I breathed an audible sigh of relief. It was as if God himself had caught me. If there is such a thing as actually feeling the peace of God wash over you, I sensed it.

From that day on I knew I didn't have to suffer such anxiety. I knew I didn't have to buy into whatever the enemy told me. My mind was mine! And for someone like me, this knowledge merited a chorus of hallelujahs to the Lamb of God!

And so I moved on. Not always immediately victorious, but always on the winning side. Each time I started to get a crazy thought, I stopped it and started thinking about something else. Each time the enemy whispered death, I shouted life. And not a life vested in this world but in the everlasting. This is, after all, what I live for.

I so love the Lord. He gave me power over my mind and authority over my enemy so that the view could change. And it did. And it does. And it forever will!

But that's not all. I'm learning now to speak these victories audibly.

You see, logically our mouths and behavior will follow our minds. So after we fight for our mind, we have to control what we say. Time after time the Bible cautions us about the power of words. In the book of Proverbs we are told, "Death and life are in the power of the tongue, and those who love it will eat its fruit" (18:21 NKJV).

Even words and thoughts that seem relatively innocuous have great power in determining reality. Whether we speak positively into our lives or we speak death, our words help to determine the outcome.

I truly believe that if our thoughts and words are filled with contention and strife, that is what we will experience. If our thoughts and words are filled with happiness and joy, that is what we will experience. And so we must be more aware of the things we speak into our own lives. We have to start recognizing when we are speaking negative words into our lives and the lives of others.

I know a woman about seventy-five years old who has been a faithful believer for many years. Two of her sons are addicted to drugs. Of course, her heart breaks for them, and I believe her when she tells me she prays for them every day. She prays for God to break the curse, because otherwise "they will die on that stuff," she says.

I believe her words reflect the fear in her heart, but they speak death regarding her sons' addictions. This is not the will of our Father. He wants us to speak life!

———

A few years ago I underwent many different types of therapy in an effort to learn to successfully manage PTSD and the panic attacks I was having. One thing that helped me most was a form of talk therapy known as Cognitive-Behavioral Therapy (CBT). It aims to reacquaint the patient with the pre-panic self. During the course of treatment, the patient learns to "talk back" to thoughts that perpetuate anxiety.

Talk back!

It was difficult at first to sit peacefully in different situations and ignore my mind's disquieting chatter. Hearing myself think my plane would explode on take-off, I would force myself to respond, "Not this time." My mind would tell me the devil was going to take over my family, and I would respond, "Not on my watch."

Talk back!

I am not angry; I am a child of God! (see 1 John 5:1)

I am not going astray; my steps are ordered of the Lord. (see Psalm 37:23)

I am not fighting this fight alone. The angel of the Lord encamps about me to protect me and deliver me. (see Psalm 34:7)

Many are the afflictions of the righteous, but the Lord delivers them out of them all. (see Psalm 34:19)

Today is the best day of my life. (see Romans 8:28; Proverbs 4:18)

I began asking the Lord Jesus Christ to help me develop a positive thought life. Over time, by immersing myself in His Word, praying, and talking back, I discovered I *could* control the way I think and focus on certain thoughts while rejecting others.

At first it took quite a bit of practice. I even learned to anticipate where my mind was about to take me and then took control of that direction. Talking to myself was easy for me and quickly became a good habit.

I encourage you to try this at home or anywhere else you find your mind ill at ease. But bear in mind that my experiences and advice may not be for everyone. In my opinion, however, all of this is quite simple and potentially life-changing. It was for me.

I came through declaring that I would never again be imprisoned by my own mind. And never again would I allow my enemy's lies to have power over my mind. I also drew inspiration from a book by Don Gossett, *What You Say Is What You Get*. He suggested people write down a "never again" list. Mine is below, which you are free to adapt to fit your own life. Even better, develop your own list. The objective is to regain control of your mind by living in victory, talking back, and declaring the Word of God, rightly applying it to your situations. May you be blessed in this!

My "Never Again" List

1. Never again will I believe that I am not attractive, because I am fearfully and wonderfully made. God's works are beautiful. (Psalm 139:14)

2. Never again will I fret about being single or feel lonely, because I have learned in whatever situation I am to be content. (Philippians 4:11)

3. Never again will I walk guilt-ridden or ashamed of my past sins, because I am forgiven (Colossians 1:13–14). Therefore, there is now no condemnation to those who are in Christ Jesus. (Romans 8:1)

4. Never again will I walk in any line with addiction or trauma, because I am delivered from the powers of darkness (Colossians 1:13). Whom the Son sets free is free indeed.

5. Never again will I worry about my loved ones' lives, because my entire household will be saved. (Acts 16:31)

6. Never again will I give the devil control of my mind or dwell on sinful and destructive thoughts, because God has given me authority to bring every thought into captivity. (2 Corinthians 10:5)

7. Never again will I allow the enemy to convince me that he has victory over me, because greater is He that is within me than he that is in the world. (1 John 4:4)

8. Never again will I say I can't do something, because I can do all things through Christ which strengthens me. (Philippians 4:13)

9. Never again will I measure my life's success by worldly value, because it is nothing compared to the value of my soul. (Matthew 16:26)

10. Never again will I worry over my finances, because my God shall supply all of my needs according to His riches in glory by Christ Jesus. (Philippians 4:19)

11. Never again will I give my soul over to my temper, because I know that my anger does NOT achieve or represent the righteousness of God. (James 1:20)

12. Never again will I wonder if God answers my prayers, because the prayers of a righteous man avail much. (James 5:16)

13. Never again will I confess curses or bad luck for myself or those I love, because Christ has redeemed us from the curse of the law . . . that we might receive the promise of the Spirit through faith. (Galatians 3:13–14)

14. Never again will I allow my flesh to drive my passions, because the Lord has said to me, "Though your sins are like scarlet, they shall be as white as snow." (Isaiah 1:18)

15. Never again will I fear what happens next in life, because I am strong and courageous—not afraid or terrified—for the Lord God goes with me. (Deuteronomy 31:6)

16. Never again will I allow life to stop me from living, because I am hard pressed on every side but not crushed, perplexed but not in despair, persecuted but not abandoned, struck down but not destroyed! (2 Corinthians 4:8–9)

Remember, the confession of your mouth in many situations determines the outcome. *Talk back!*

25

...AND THE MEDITATIONS OF MY HEART

MY BOOK OF PRAYERS

My Never Again List, accompanied by powerful, applicable Scriptures, has really been a great help to me in the last few years. That and other terrific little jewels, which I call my spiritual cheat sheets, are helping me live in peace and freedom. I find that I'm not so much swimming against the tide of life anymore as I'm standing, bracing myself, and riding the waves.

I am having the time of my life, living by what the Lord has provided through His written Word. And as I do, my relationship with Him matures and begins to look more like Father and daughter as opposed to big God, little god. Some of the huge things that I was once so passionate about are becoming less big, even tiny. Honestly, laughable.

For example, there was once a time when I wasn't a big fan of writing down my prayers. Recording them seemed a little rehearsed to me, irreverent. I wanted my conversations with God, or prayer life, to be fresh and pleasing to the Lord. And I felt that in order for that to be true, I had to think up the pretty "thus and thou" prayers spontaneously.

Then one day I was reflecting on a few Scriptures and taking a few notes. I paid attention to what the book of Psalms actually was. In particular, Psalm 19:14: "Let the words of my mouth and the meditation of my heart be pleasing in your sight, O Lord, my Rock and my Redeemer," and Psalm 49:3: "My mouth shall speak wisdom, and the meditation of my heart shall give understanding."

The Psalms are actually prayers! The psalmist is actually meditating on his words to the Lord and writing them down—another *duh* moment in the life of Leslie Haskin.

I know that for some, the mention of the word *meditation* brings to mind someone sitting on the floor, legs crossed, eyes closed, fingers forming a steeple, spending hours ignoring the world. But meditation doesn't have to look like that.

The word itself simply means to reflect upon, ponder, or engage in contemplation. So when we are meditating on God's Word, we read it, think about it, and ponder it. As we go about doing other things, it sinks into our hearts, and we'll dwell on it some more, and so on. Psalm 1:2 says of the believer's life: "But his delight is in the law of the Lord, and on His law he meditates day and night."

I've been meditating now for many years. I began writing prayers and psalms about four years ago, and it's actually very refreshing. In fact, I have a little prayer book where I record the names of people who have asked me to pray for them as well as a reminder of some general prayers throughout the day.

Today I have an entire notebook of prayers. When I look back on some of the more specific ones, I am amazed at how many He has answered, particularly those regarding Safe HUGS (an agency that helps victims of domestic abuse). It is uplifting to me, because when I look at them, I can actually recall what was in my heart at the time that I wrote down the prayer. Most times what I recall is that He consistently ignores my words and answers the prayer of my heart.

While they are all personal, a few are more intimate than others. And even though I am not completely comfortable sharing these with you, it is what the Lord has asked of me. It is so that you might see the similarity of our hearts.

As I said before, I'm working on being immediately obedient to the Lord. These are the meditations of my heart:

• My *Psalm to the Lord*

Lord of life and love, fill me with all of you; delight yourself in my hopes to be like you; let me rest in your grace and favor, and awaken to your kisses of mercy. Amen.

• A *Prayer for Forgiveness*

Forgive me, Father, if my life has become a marketplace rather than a gift offering of worship to you. If my love has turned inward, selfishly thanking you for what you have done from my own vainglory, wash me and sit me down. Search my heart, Lord, and know me. Forgive me for the sins I have knowingly committed and those that I am unaware of. Give to me only what I am truly in need of so that I will never again find comfort or security in the material. Guide my footsteps that I would not stray from you, hold my hands that I would not fold them to other gods, and turn me upside down that I will forever seek your face. Amen.

• My *Prayer for the Church*

Father of Creation, thank you for the miracle of your plans and all that you have promised. And as we live, give us unclouded eyes and freedom from haste. Give us hearts that see by faith what a seed can become that we might freely share our faith and hope with those in need; your vision for change unadulterated by denominations, your unsurpassed love unchanged by tradition. Help us to understand the growth is for the body and not the pews. And help us, Father, those who are willing, to be constant in prayer until your return. Amen.

• *Morning Prayer*

Holy Father, thank you for daybreak and another opportunity to do what you have designed me for. This morning I dedicate myself to you all over again and I make the conscious decision to be your servant, not just your volunteer. I will go where you lead me. I give you my love, my heart, my mind, my arms, my feet, my hands, and my own will. This day I renew my dedication to serve you wholly, by holding my worship to you as my highest value. Receive my prayer as worship. As I face the challenges within this day, Lord, give me wisdom to notice the temptations that come my way so that with an honest heart I might struggle but not surrender. Give me strength to walk away. I hope today to walk in surrender to you, Father. Grant me the gift of an intimate sense of your presence throughout the day. And be careful with my Eliot; he needs your guidance. Amen.

• *Afternoon Prayer*

Father, continue to grant me the gift of your strength today. Help me to be a light that shines for you. Help me to continue to walk in service to you. And remember Eliot, Lord. He needs your direction. Amen.

• *Evening Prayer*

Thank you, Father, that I still belong to you. Thank you for a day that was filled with wonderful things and opportunities. Help me to reflect honestly on what was accomplished and what was left undone. Humble me in your service, so that tomorrow I can pursue with enthusiasm those things that you have called for me to complete.

Now, Father, grant me rest with no regrets. Forgive me if I have sinned against you. And speak into Eliot's heart your love and direction for him. I offer this day completed now to you, for your glory alone. Amen.

• *Sunday Morning Prayer*

This is the day that you have made, and I will rejoice and be glad in it! Master, this morning I wake up within your Sabbath rest, which brings a new flavor to life each time the sun rises on it. Today more than any other day, impress upon my heart the severity of holiness and sacrifice offerings. Cause all of my actions today to be pleasing in your sight and receive all I do today as worship. As I enter the sanctuary, help me to remember the holiness of it, and to regard it as you have instructed. Help me, Father, to direct my praise fully focused on your goodness and not others around me. Receive me, Father, into your house, as I receive you once again into my heart. I honor you this day, and every day that will follow. Amen.

• *Prayer for My Children*

Dear God, my children are your children. Your love for them is a trillion times more than I can ever even know, so can we agree to keep them from the perils of the world, the lies of the enemy, and from hellfire? Bring them closer to you, in a relationship and in love. Grant them in their lives, God, all that is needed and necessary to accomplish this, and I will try to stay out of your way. Amen.

• *Prayer for My Family*

I love my family, and I have hope that we will all be saved; yes, even my entire household. Only you, God, are holy. You are the Father of us all. Draw your children to yourself. Walk through the generations of my parents' blood and save, heal, deliver, set free, and again, Father, save. Amen.

• *Prayer for My Friends*

Thank you that you have given me friends who care and love me. Help me to be a friend to them as well. Amen.

• *Prayer for My Fears*

Lord, please don't let me let you down! Amen.

• *Prayer for My Lonely Heart*

Lord, I'm so lonely today. But sometimes I'm not sure if I want a husband or just want to feel less lonely. Either way, please help my heart. Know, God, I am gladly on this journey that you have called me to. Do not remove me from this place. And even though I know that you are here with me, I feel the need to be held. My heart is breaking for my own self, and I would give so much just to have one full night of sleep. Nevertheless, search my heart and my soul. Ignore the words of my mouth and give me what I need—whatever solution settles my heart and quiets the loneliness; I pray you give it to me according to your riches in glory. Then help me, Lord, to feel your presence more today, because I really need it. Amen.

• *Prayer for the Holy Spirit of God*

Dear Lord, I thank you for your Holy Spirit that you have given to the world, so that we can know you more intimately through His leading. Forgive us, Lord, for the offenses we have already committed against Him, and help us, Father, not to offend or grieve your Holy Spirit. Amen.

• *Prayer for the World*

Father, let a portion of your love enter our hearts today, that we might be able to pray in earnest for a dying world. Help me to be a light that leads others to you. Open the eyes of the world, and draw your people nearer to you. Heal the brokenhearted. Send deliverance, set souls free, and bring peace. And most of all, Lord, make your love evident to those who truly seek you and your salvation. Then return for your church. Amen.

• *Prayer for Those I Serve*

Lord, use my hands to give to those who are suffering. Surround them with your love. Reach beyond their darkness and heal them in body and soul. Enlighten them that they might come to know the gentle and enduring peace of your Spirit. Save, restore, and keep them, Father, as they journey home. Amen.

• *Prayer for Peace*

Father, my family and friends and people I don't know are hurting, suffering, and looking for you. Give them peace! In this moment, grant them a soul's restoration and complete rest. Amen.

• *Prayer Before I Read My Bible*

Father, mine is a thick but receptive heart. Penetrate it with the light of your Word. Open the eyes of my heart so that I can see clearly the wisdom of your teaching and follow you with eagerness. As I read today, impress upon me true reverence for your words so that I am strengthened to conquer my flesh and pursue a spiritual way of life, exhibiting behavior that is most pleasing to you. Thank you that you hear and answer me. Amen.

Teacher, help me to understand fully what you are trying to teach me. Blind my eyes to my own understanding and give me full clarity within you that I might write your words on the tables of my heart. Amen.

• *Prayer for Myself*

Dear God, I need your help. Help me to remember that I am not here for myself, but that I am called as a servant for the sake of your love, to make this love real and manifest before other people. Help me to fulfill this task in the way I write, speak, sing, and bring glory to your name.

Remind me daily of your great love, how it has always been present with me in the past, how it guides me now, and will be with me throughout eternity. If I am weak now, let me rest as Elijah did; if I am confused, give me wisdom as you gave to Moses; if I am full of fleshly desire, purge me as you have done for all those who have opened up to you. My desire is to live pleasing in your eyes, now and forever in your presence.

Father, as the days go by and this journey progresses, I get a little tired from time to time. I wish that I could say that I am never tired or never questioning, but that would be a lie. I am often tired. Will you lend me your strength? Today, I lost my temper more than a few times, and my mouth followed the poor example that my attitude set. Forgive me. And teach me to be more like you. Remind me not to judge the call on my life, but to humble myself and submit myself to it. Help me to respond immediately to your voice and not fight back so much. Forgive me, Father. I really do love you.

I thank you, Father, that you hear me, and because you hear me you answer, and for your answer to my prayers, I thank you, even now and throughout eternity. Amen.

• *Prayer for Safe HUGS*

Father, bless this ministry with direction and clarity of purpose. But do not allow me to govern it or put it in a box. Bless this ministry that it would touch many lives and lead those lives to your definition of worth and worthy. Take me to the streets and on the road to help restore families, heal them, and subtract people from the number of those counted homeless and forgotten. I pray, Father, that you would raise up my voice and give me words to speak. Give me the courage to go where others won't, and then send me, I pray. Amen.

• *Prayer When I Am Feeling Alone*

Father, I need your Spirit. I can't hear you. Are you whispering to me? Amen.

• *Prayer for Eliot*

Please, Father, remember my son, Eliot—by any means necessary. Amen.

• *Prayer to Show Love*

Creator God, you are the God of Abraham and David. Only you are holy and only you can heal a dying world. Only you can shine a never-ending light into a darkness that runs deep. Only your love can restore places and things that I once believed were lost forever. Father, I come asking that you make your love clear to everyone. Cause your love, Lord, to reach those who seek you now and bring them new life. Let me be a part of your shared love. Let me go into the world, even as you have asked me to do, and be your outstretched arms. Help me to open my heart up more, giving your love more room to fill every space that I occupy, reaching out into the community and beyond. Raise up others as well, Father, who would not sacrifice your truth for the world's favor or your holiness for modern culture.

And then fully engage us in warfare. Fit us with full armor that we might put it on and put the enemy under our feet. Cause us to face with courage the war that we have been called to, quenching the fires of darkness. Also, Father, teach me how to love you *more*. Teach me to walk every day upright and holy, guarding my trust in your faithfulness and every grace I have ever known.

Give me, and help me to be mindful of, that mustard seed of faith that I am to plant in others. Cause me to plant it freely, without obligation but with love and honor. Then keep me humbled in the stillness of your love, wherein lies the strength that makes me immovable in the face of danger, threats, fears, seductions, and the present cruelty of the human heart, even my own. For all of this, Father, I give you thanks. Then, Master, I pray that the words of my mouth and the meditation of my heart would be acceptable in your sight, O Lord, my strength and my redeemer. I praise you! Amen.

And He answered their prayers, because they trusted in Him (1 Chronicles 5:20).

26

JUST DO IT!

FOR THE LOVE OF GOD

"If I have a faith that can move mountains, but have not love, I am nothing."

This Scripture is taken from First Corinthians. The thirteenth chapter describes what love is, and I gotta tell ya, I love it. It's beautiful, simple, and straightforward.

When I was a young girl I collected those "Love is . . ." stickers. I had at least a thousand of them. I loved their simplistic definitions of love, things like "Love is giving him the last slice of cake" or "Love is a short walk with her after a long workout." Even today, I love *love*. I enjoy reading about it, thinking of it, believing in it, and living it, don't you?

It feels good to see a child's face fill with joy in response to something you've done, or to have a puppy jump into your arms when you walk into the room. It's an amazing feeling to see love in the eyes of someone you love or to show love to someone who needs it.

And then there's the love of God.

What feels better than experiencing the peaceful and soothing presence of the Lord—rich, full, and restorative? What state of mind can surpass that moment when you know that God is real—beyond measure or doubt?

I know of nothing better. For in these moments, the assurance that God loves us without need of reciprocation or condition is awesome! Now, I know that the concept of love without reciprocation is a little hard for our small minds to grasp; many of us have been taught it isn't possible. But the truth is, God's love IS love. It is without self-interest. It is pure. It is without cause or condition. It is beyond reason.

God doesn't need a reason to love us. He doesn't love us because of the good that we do or don't do. He doesn't love us only because He created us. It is simply love. It is mind-boggling, I know, but this is God! And is God not bigger than our understanding? Don't you think that if our small minds can understand Him, we are missing something?

The same then must be true about fully understanding His love. Scripture says, "God is love, and he who abides in love abides in God, and God in him" (1 John 4:16 NKJV). What a huge concept . . . a wonderful thing!

When we become Christian believers, God's love lives in us, and He expects us to love Him in the same way He loves us . . . without condition or need for reciprocation or reason. You see, just as between a man and a woman, the moment we love God for any reason—what He does for us, or gives us, or delivers us from—it is no longer love.

"Love is patient, love is kind and is not jealous; love does not brag and is not arrogant, does not act unbecomingly; it does not seek its own, is not provoked, does not take into account a wrong suffered, does not rejoice in unrighteousness, but rejoices with the truth; bears all things, believes all things, hopes all things, endures all things" (1 Corinthians 13:4–7 NKJV).

So let me ask you, do you love God? Do you love Him like that? Do you love Him enough to disregard the present condition of your life in favor of the condition of your heart? Enough to gracefully accept life as it is? God wants us to love Him for who He is, not for what He can do for us. The relationship He desires of us presupposes a two-way relationship in which love engages heart, soul, mind, and strength. Perhaps Jesus said it best when He said, "Love the Lord your God with all your heart and with all your soul and with all your mind" (Matthew 22:37). Every facet of your personality, character, actions and reactions, affection, intellect, and will should be touched and transformed by God's love for you and your love for God.

Do you love Him like that?

Often we live our relationship with God under the heading of being a Christian. And our Christianity becomes more of a responsibility than an act of love. We talk about how *much* we love the Lord until a quantifiable love becomes what we understand and what we teach. We so easily fall into a reciprocal way of thinking— looking for ways God shows His love for us and how we can show our love for Him. So when life throws us any ol' curve ball, we can't understand how God could allow it. But that's not biblical. Life's varying conditions have nothing at all to do with God's love for us, and should have nothing to do with how much we love God. In Jeremiah 31:3, God says, "I have loved you with an everlasting love." My friends, the word *everlasting* is neither quantitative nor quantifying. It is without measure—vast. And how do you measure vastness? Like the wind or molecules floating in space?

God's love is real love, continuous and intentional. And we must allow it to become our love as well, adjusting our focus from an individual or self-centered standpoint to a higher perspective. From that point of view, our relationship with Him, which is based on our love for Him and His for us, keeps us grounded, safe, secure, hopeful, and content.

I think that's how Paul learned to be content in every situation—by loving God more than comfort. Nothing distracted him or kept him from making his love for God foremost in his life. Paul declared that nothing would separate him from the love of God.

Man, to live like that . . . to trust and hope and love like that. That's the kind of love that changes things, and people too. That's the love that says, "Bring it on, world. Tell the lies, spread the rumors, send the stress, even take my life." "Hit me with your best shot, enemy—busy up my days, steal my job. I have found real love, and nothing will ever separate me from God!"

A few chapters back I talked about taking my new car to the dealership to get a simple tire change and having to wait for hours in that place. Well, what I didn't mention then is relevant now.

During my wait I met a young agnostic Jewish man. He told me he was married and had children. As our conversation progressed, he let me know that he and his wife were "spiritual but not religious." He explained that they were choosing to raise their children with the concept that all religions contain some bit of truth, and the journey through life is to gather those truths in order to live an upstanding and moral life.

Of course, I don't share his beliefs, but I didn't outwardly disagree with him. I have learned not to try to prove truth, for truth reveals itself.

When the young man asked me about my beliefs, I explained that I am a devout follower of Jesus Christ. He reiterated that he was spiritual but not religious, and then went on to explain that he rejects the idea of religion because it forces people to behave in a specific manner with no real proof of reward or punishment.

While I wanted to politely change the subject, my desire to share Christ kept me talking. I told him that being a Christian is not ritualistic—not the result of an ethical choice or a lofty idea but of an encounter with a God who gives life new horizons and faith to look beyond this temporal existence.

The young man sat up in his seat, as if readying himself for the dance, and challenged me. "Do you think any other religions would satisfy you or give you the same feelings as Christianity?"

I smiled, opened my mouth, and the Holy Spirit answered in my stead. "Before I answer, may I ask you a question?" He said yes.

"Do you really love your wife?"

His face assumed a stern look as he answered emphatically, "Yes."

Then I asked, "Do you think someone else could satisfy you or give you the same feelings as she?" A smile came to his face as he told me that he'd never heard it explained that way before.

You see, if we really love God, then love is enough. If we really understand and embrace the depth of God's love for us—if we know in our knowers that God's love is expressed in the life, death, and resurrection of Jesus—we cannot help but live in this spirit of love. And this love flows down into our relationships and situations, even to the point of proving that God is one God. Our heart, soul, mind, and strength are transformed by love—fully engaged in everyday living, turning every circumstance of life into a triumph.

"Who shall separate us from the love of Christ? Shall tribulation, or distress, or persecution, or famine, or nakedness, or peril, or sword? . . . Yet in all these things we are more than conquerors through Him who loved us" (Romans 8:35, 37 NKJV).

27

AND NOW, HIS PRAISES!

MAKE IT GLORIOUS

Last year I went through a very difficult time. The doctors had found another small tumor and also several polyps in my nasal passages. I was experiencing migraine headaches and vertigo, and if that wasn't enough, I started seeing my age in my face. It was very stressful; seeing and realizing my age, that is.

I had been on the road off and on for about a week, and as usual I was fighting through my flesh to hold back the tired Leslie in exchange for the "Leslie of God's design."

I was in San Diego for a revival, and after the service and dinner with the pastor, I finally made it back to my hotel at about eleven that night. (That's two AM for New Yorkers!)

I stepped about five feet into the hotel lobby and was met by a man who had apparently heard my message of deliverance and decided that he needed to speak with me one-on-one. He wanted me to come to his home and pray for him so that the devil would leave. The man was convinced that ghosts were haunting his home. His face looked desperate.

I sat on the sofa next to him and listened to his stories of torment and torture. He wanted to be free.

Now, as much as I wanted to strap on my demon-slayer cape and run to his aid, I knew that God is a God of order and would not have me in a situation without a strong covering. I explained to the man, whom I now knew as Steven, that God is not limited by our walls, and that if he really believed I could help him, that meant he had to know God would help him.

I made a decision to pray for him and to praise God with him right then and there. I read a few Scripture verses and started praising God.

As I began, "Praise you, Lord," he joined me in a rather wimpy, unconvincing tone. The devil started mocking me via my own thoughts: *"You know he doesn't believe things will change! He doesn't really mean it. Give up!"* As I persisted, doggedly pressing in to the God I knew through years of experience to be good, loving, and real, the man's tone began to change.

I noticed at first a nervous sound came into his voice as he started saying, "Thank you, Jesus. Jesus, you are merciful. Have mercy!"

I continued praising. I opened my eyes and noticed the young lady at the front desk had quietly joined us. I was getting pumped! As I continued, my voice began to get stronger and more confident, and I began to remember appropriate Scriptures and use them.

After what felt like ten minutes (which was actually thirty minutes), I was in full shout, and the hotel lobby was being flooded with praises coming so fast that my mouth could hardly keep up with them. Steven was speaking in tongues with tears in his eyes.

The Lord came through that hotel lobby and brought deliverance from an oppressive spirit.

By the time he left the lobby, Steven was walking in victory.

The Lord reminded me the next day and throughout the week of what happens when we praise God. At the name of Jesus, every knee bows to His authority (Philippians 2:10). By His name and through praise, our spirit enters into fellowship and intimacy with the Lord, taking us into the realm of the supernatural and into the presence of God.

Now, allow me to pause for a minute and explain something: *Ruach* (Ru-ah) is Hebrew for *breath,* and represents the spirit—literally. It is the breath of God, His essence, and it is synonymous with life. The root of the word is related to words meaning "voice," "thunder," and "wind"—even if He only breathes. And so when we were created by God, it was *ruach* that put life into us; when He anoints our lives, it is with *ruach*; and because His Word declares that He dwells in the praises of His people, when we enter into His presence in worship, it is *ruach* that engulfs us.

As we praise God, the manifest presence of the Holy Spirit, His anointing, or His breath, brings a change to the atmosphere around us, enabling faith, prophecy, healing, miracles, deliverance, and more to take place. Isaiah 10:27 says, "The yoke will be destroyed because of the anointing" (NKJV).

When we praise God in earnest, which means focusing on Him rather than our issues, ourselves, and our situations, amazing things happen. He looses the chains that bind up our souls! He breaks the yokes that keep us burdened with sin, and His Holy Spirit brings comfort and pours out deliverance!

And so, once again, I have no idea where you are in your life, but let me encourage you to call on the name of the Lord. Because "where the Spirit of the Lord is, there is freedom" (2 Corinthians 3:17). Get up from wherever you are and begin to praise Him.

I know it might feel a little awkward at first, and this might be a little too "out there" for some. But at the risk of all that, I believe that if you take a few minutes to stand your ground and praise Him until the walls fall, the chains break, and the enemy is under your feet, every mountain, every chain, every stronghold will come down!

I hear from Steven (the man in the hotel lobby) from time to time, and he is doing very well. He has been gifted with joy, and on the occasions when I am blessed to hear from him praises to the Lord, I'm encouraged to praise God myself. I am committed to encourage you to praise Him as well, and that we all will make His praise glorious!

Now may the God of all grace, who called us to His eternal glory by Christ Jesus, perfect, establish, strengthen, and settle you, even through praise!

28

GOD HAS NOT FORGOTTEN ABOUT YOU

IT REALLY IS A WONDERFUL LIFE

Life is not lived alone. We are a great mass of interconnected pieces, each needing the other for support, encouragement, and emotional stability. Every life touches another life. Every choice impacts another. And in the middle of it all is God—up close, personal, and moving the trillions of living pieces around us to guarantee that the consequences of our shortsightedness still work together for our eventual and eternal good.

Life is not a linear highway that moves us from start to finish, as some of us have come to believe. It is instead *the* great adventure that takes us to and from in an unpredictable loop where the meaning of it all, reconciliation with God our Father, rests at its core. There is nothing bigger than that!

And so I guess that brings us right back to where we started, about Goliath—representing the hugeness of not only enduring but living this happy, sad, and wonderfully complicated life. And in light of what's real and lasting, agree with me that life itself isn't so big; it's the living that increases in size!

Complete living! Shalom living! Trusting-in-God living— intentionally being engaged in an all-encompassing life! For this, my friends, is what makes us who we are! *"Hallelujah to the Lamb of God!"* This, my friends, is what gives us the assurance even through the darkest night and the lowest valley that God has not forgotten about us.

You are today who you are because of every person, every experience, and every thought that God has allowed and connected to bring about His redemption plan in your life. *Perfect.*

Now, with that said, if you consider what you've learned from your life experiences, and if it was yours to change, what lessons would you *unlearn?* Who would you rather be?

Knowing what you now know, that every person in your life has added something to your makeup, and all of your life experiences are shared by someone else as well, are these experiences yours alone to take back? What learning would you deny someone else? Which person in your collective world would you eliminate and whose life would you change?

Do you remember the movie *It's a Wonderful Life?* The actor Jimmy Stewart plays a small-town businessman by the name of George Bailey. George has spent his entire life giving of himself to the people of Bedford Falls. He has always longed to travel but never had the opportunity. Measuring his success by material things, George spent his adult life trying to "get ahead" and fighting the power of his greedy nemesis, Mr. Potter, who wants to take over the entire town and force all the people to live dependent on him.

The only thing that stands in Potter's way is George's modest company, a building-and-loan firm, which was founded by his father.

Then on Christmas Eve, when everyone is celebrating the success of the company and the heroics of George's brother Harry, George's Uncle Billy mislays $8,000 while intending to deposit it in the bank—the same $8,000 the building and loan needs to stay afloat.

Somehow, Mr. Potter finds the misplaced money, hides it from Billy, and calls the bank examiner to report the shortage. George, finding out about the money, realizes that he will be held responsible, be sent to jail, and lose the company, and Potter will take over. Then George, believing somehow that his family would be better off with him dead, decides to jump off a bridge.

Now, here is the best part: "But the prayers of a righteous man avail much." George's family and friends, realizing that George is missing, begin praying for him. Their prayers result in a gentle angel named Clarence coming to earth to help George.

Clarence shows George how much his life means by showing him how the world would be without him. It's not pretty. His cheerful, friendly town of Bedford Falls is dreary and impoverished, sunk in sex and sin, and those whom George loves most are dead, ruined, or miserable.

Eventually George makes the decision to live and returns home to find that he's been bailed out by the charity of his friends. He realizes that he has touched many people in a positive way and that his life has truly been a wonderful one. The movie ends with all of George's friends and family at his home celebrating his victory. Then Harry makes a toast to his brother George: "The richest man in Bedford Falls."

At a high-level view, George's story might look a little bleak. None of the plans that he had for his life were met. Even after divine intervention, he was still stuck in the muck and mire and rut of boring ol' Bedford Falls. He was still trapped in a job that he didn't like, still living in the shadow of the heroics of others, and still eventually having to deal with Potter.

And Potter, in his wickedness, was unchanged and had successfully stolen $8,000.

But on a deeper level, George's story is perfectly inspirational. Because if it is about anything, it is an example of the connectedness and interdependencies of our lives and how God uses each of us to reveal the things in life that we should aspire to, those of eternal value.

George came to understand that God's plan for him was too big to be delivered within the confines of travel and being an architect. God's plan involved George helping to keep hundreds of people from homelessness, suicide, degradation, prostitution, bitterness, and ultimately, eternal damnation.

God had not forgotten about George in that old town. In fact, He was remembering all of the people there. God had not overlooked George's desires. He saw the true desires of his heart: living beyond the ordinary, being spectacular, and adding value to the lives of those around him.

These are the things that we should look at when the world tells us that we are alone, that we've failed, or that God has somehow forgotten about us. These are the things that we should remember when we are asked by God to live within a situation that on the surface may look like there is no earthly reason for it to be what it is.

Recently a friend was in an accident on the highway near my home. She and her husband were riding a motorcycle, and a truck fishtailed into them and knocked them from their bike. They were airlifted to an area hospital where the doctors immediately performed surgery.

The family, the church, and even people throughout the community came to the hospital to offer support. They came to the church, where people prayed, begging God for miraculous healing. Here's the prayer that I recorded in my prayer journal: *On behalf of these children who need their parents, Father, I ask that you provide a miracle today. For those who are watching but don't know that you are a miracle-working God, that they would come to know that you are God.*

The next morning, I got the news that Cindy had passed away. Her husband died soon after. They left behind five children, all under the age of eighteen. It was heartbreaking.

I met Cindy's mom for the first time about five months later at a women's weekend retreat. I hugged her and shared with her how sorry I was for her loss. Then I asked about the children. This is what I was told almost verbatim: "Those children had good, loving Christian parents for as long as they had them. They have a family who cares for them now and a wonderful God who loves and looks after them always."

Wow. Her words shared a trust in God that inspired me. The bottom line for those children is everybody's bottom line. We may or may not know specifically why God allows what He allows, but we know beyond any doubt that it is absolutely for our eternal good.

We understand now that God doesn't set us on a path to heaven and then forget about us. Nor does He watch from a distance. We can't earn His attention or deserve His love. He gives it freely because of who He is and who we are to Him. There is no secret prayer that we need to pray and no checklist that qualifies us in His eyes for a response.

God loves us. He is interactive, loving, and present with us no matter what our life circumstances are. Isaiah 49:15–16 says, "Can a woman forget her nursing child, and not have compassion on the son of her womb? Surely they may forget, yet I will not forget you. See, I have inscribed you on the palms of my hands" (NKJV). God has not forgotten about you.

What more is there beyond this other than to live? So as life happens, live it. Stay faithful to your relationship with God and just keep living! Keep going to church, keep talking *and* listening to God, keep praising and keep striving for the spectacular. Keep riding the ups and the downs, expecting the unexpected; keep embracing the transformations, and keep on loving Him.

In the interim, whatever is yours to be had, you will have. God won't let you miss His plans. Set aside some time in your secret closet to spend with Him and then wait. Read your Bible constantly as a reminder of what things you should say as you "talk back," and wait. Record your favorite Scriptures and place them around your house, commit them to your heart, and then wait.

Wait on God. He won't let you down, and His timing is always perfect. My mom would say, "He may not come when you want Him, but He's always right on time" (see Ecclesiastes 3:11; Isaiah 40:31; James 1:3–4).

It's so true. He's always on time for us—on time remembering us and the covenant that He has established with us. On time converting us, uniting us to Christ, and bringing to fulfillment all the wonderful promises about our future living: a new and better life in a new and better body on a new and better earth.

So what does it matter then which way is up, as long as you are along for the ride? Because when our life here on earth is over, we'll leave behind little more than a stone in the ground and a whisper to the world. We might as well loudly proclaim to the watchers, to those who seek truth, and to the doubters that despite the lies and plans to destroy us, we chose to love and to be part of the bride of Jesus the Christ, who likes to shake things up.

Let us declare that we have lived every minute of all that Christ has allowed to come our way—with pleasure.

As for me, I lean back into life, spread my arms and open my heart, allowing all of life's remaining mysteries to greet me in my soul.

And trust me, when the time comes, you won't find me kicking or sighing or fighting back. I'll close my eyes and go happily, gracefully, smiling, and real. And everyone will know that I didn't simply visit this world, I lived it! Having embraced this full journey as passionately as I could, I've lived the beauty of God's grace to the fullest. I've shared the fascination of His love from coast to coast, and I've made of my life something spectacular and real—even if only in His eyes and mine.

And when I arrive in heaven with the lyrics to comfortable music in my mouth, I'll tend toward the party people . . . and breathe.

29

The Celebration of Overcoming

An Invitation

The sounds of happy folks will fill the air. Horns will play loudly, and the thump of the bass guitar is going to penetrate the soul. Folk or jazz or some spiritual music like that will be up-tempo, making joyful noises and causing people to dance. Just one of many celebrations of overcoming taking place in the new Earth, this will be an awesome time.

In worship to the Lord, and speaking freely of His grace on earth, polite partygoers will help themselves to frozen punch, Kool-Aid, hors d'oeuvres, and brownies while telling their individual stories as the band plays on.

The sounds of laughter spreading for blocks will drown the sounds of the natural nighttime. None of the neighbors complain; they're all there. Lining the walls, standing in open doorways, sitting on steps, and typical of how we do, gathering in the kitchen.

Martha, Mary's sister, is puttering around the stove, raving about her cooking skills and her new strawberry punch. Mary is serving up blueberry, strawberry, and banana pancakes, while my friend Joyce is perfecting just the right blend of walnuts and chocolate in her world-famous brownies. Try them if ever you get the chance.

The front of the house is just as meaty. In one corner of the dining room, Jonah stands talking with a few of my new friends from Louisiana. Comparing notes on just how high the waters can rise, they wave their arms about descriptively, stamp their feet, and jump, all in an effort to make their point—until Noah walks by, just by chance.

Jonah looks at Katrina, they pause a minute and then laugh. Noah just stands there, a bit confused by the whole thing, and asks, "What?"

It's this way throughout the house. Conversation is certainly not lacking and is being had by all.

Daniel talks confines with Mandela, while Moses argues civil rights with King. My mom grabs a microphone and joins that famous band from the *Titanic* that never quits. And the band plays on.

Me, I'll be running through the house, being the perfect little hostess and trying my best to convince everyone that my great escape was planned from day one.

The house will be decorated with fresh-cut roses, fragrant peonies, and tall ice sculptures that rival the works of Michelangelo.

It isn't long until the party segues down the back steps and poolside. I continue my discussion on lyrical writing styles with my friend Paul, and he laughs. I speak about my great escape and Moses looks my way. And just about the time when I begin to speak of the many sacrifices I made for the kingdom, my Beloved walks in.

He politely touches my shoulder and smiles. That's what I like about you, my little one, you're never too shy to speak . . .

It's going to happen, you know. The end is really the beginning; and one day you and I will actually be in heaven at this very celebration of overcoming, looking back, and reminding each other of this very moment in time. How cool will that be? Imagine talking about this, from there.

That look ahead makes our present journey a moot point . . . it makes it worth it!

And with that being the case, I cannot close this book without taking the opportunity to invite you to come to know my Beloved as I do and join us at the Celebration.

He is Jesus of Nazareth. Christ, the Messiah, who sacrificed everything so that you could be reconciled with God and live with Him forever in heaven. I'm sure that you've heard at least a million times that He loves you, but perhaps you are hearing for the first time that He also wants you to love Him.

Getting to know God and His character requires spending time in His Word as well as in His presence. The closer you get to Him, the more you'll love Him.

Will you take the time to get to know Him, and fall in love? I guess the real question is: Have you had enough grief in your life? Haven't you experienced enough disappointment? Have you spent much of your life waiting for that something that will make you happy and fulfilled? If so, I humbly suggest to you that that something is Someone: Jesus Christ.

Will you invite Him to show himself to you as never before? Are you willing to get to know Him? As Nana said, what do you lose by taking hold of everything?

When I met the Lord, I told Him that I didn't know Him and I didn't love Him. But that if He were so inclined, I wanted to get to know Him. And I thank God that He was so inclined! Those were the honest words of my heart, and now my heart sings, *Emmanuel, I love Him, and He knows me!*

I hesitate to tell you what exactly to pray. Know that there are no secret words or order of words, or right or wrong words, just your honest words. It is, after all, your heart that He's looking for.

And so, if you are ready to do so, speak to Him. Ask Him to be *Lord* of your life and over your circumstances. Then receive the Lord Jesus Christ as your Savior, Friend, Confidant, and Lord.

And if we don't meet here, on this soil, I'll see you at my mansion in heaven. You have a personal invitation from me to join the party! And don't worry, you won't miss the house. Mine will be the big cream-colored Victorian on the corner, where all the music is coming from. Just follow the laughter. . . .

I'll see you there!

Love Always,
Leslie D. Haskin